W9-DFJ-117

DOES THE PEAK TO PEEK PRINCIPLE REALLY WORK? JUST ASK—

RICH DeVOS AND JAY VAN ANDEL, who started with a desk and an idea and created the Amway Corporation, which has made millionaires out of policemen, teachers, and janitors . . .

Or GEORGE JOHNSON, who started out selling hair cream to Chicago barbershops and then got an idea: a hair straightener he called Afro-Sheen that made him tens of millions of dollars . . .

Or JOHN CREAN, who turned his talent for making blinds for house trailers and just $250 worth of wood and rope into the nation's number-one mobile home manufacturer, Fleetwood Enterprises . . .

Or DR. JUDY HUNTSINGER, an average home-maker, mother, and wife who listened to the Peak to Peek Principle, put it into action, and became one of America's most respected psychologists . . .

Or ROBERT H. SCHULLER, who turned a $200,000 bank loan into the magnificent $14 million, mortgage-free Crystal Cathedral. . . .

THE PEAK TO PEEK PRINCIPLE LET IT WORK FOR YOU

THE PEAK TO PEEK PRINCIPLE

Robert H. Schuller

BANTAM BOOKS
NEW YORK · TORONTO · LONDON · SYDNEY · AUCKLAND

This edition contains the complete text
of the original hardcover edition.
NOT ONE WORD HAS BEEN OMITTED.

THE PEAK TO PEEK PRINCIPLE

A Bantam Book / published by arrangement with
Doubleday

PRINTING HISTORY
Doubleday edition published 1980

Excerpts from The Hiding Place © 1971 by Corrie ten Boom and
John and Elizabeth Sherrill, published by Chosen Books.

Bantam edition / April 1990

ISBN 0-553-28378-2

Published simultaneously in the United States and Canada

Bantam Books are published by Bantam Books, a division of Bantam Doubleday
Dell Publishing Group, Inc. Its trademark, consisting of the words "Bantam
Books" and the portrayal of a rooster, is Registered in U.S. Patent and
Trademark Office and in other countries. Marca Registrada. Bantam Books,
666 Fifth Avenue, New York, New York 10103.

PRINTED IN THE UNITED STATES OF AMERICA

RAD   0 9 8 7 6 5 4 3 2 1

Contents

Introduction

In the past thirteen years I have written a number of books, published millions of copies of pamphlets, and delivered hundreds of messages to many millions of people over the television program "Hour of Power." The program is syndicated each week on over one hundred fifty television stations in the United States and Canada and on twenty stations in Australia.

In each of our "Hour of Power" messages, both printed and spoken, we have maintained that anyone can succeed if he or she makes a commitment to possibility thinking. By success we mean the achieving of a predetermined objective that makes manifest a person's chosen value system. By possibility thinking we mean that mental attitude which assumes that any objective that is noble, admirable, or beautiful can be realized even if it appears to be impossible.

Today's perceived impossibilities are turned into tomorrow's achieved possibilities when possibility thinking takes over. That's a fact!

In my files are tens of thousands of written testimonials of persons who did just that—turned perceived impossibilities into achieved possibilities by using the concepts and principles we have been communicating for a decade and a half.

In this book you'll read how I put these teachings to the acid test in my personal, professional, and family life during these years. I found that the results not only matched previously stated claims but exceeded them. In one case I saw my daughter, on the verge of death and despite the amputation of a leg, go on to achieve astounding success. In another situation I was called upon to lead our young church in a building project considered impossible.

I'll tell you stories—all true—of below-average losers who've become above-average winners by using the basic possibility-thinking management principle I call the Peak to Peek Principle. I'm referring to:

• academic dropouts who started over and earned advanced degrees.

• wage earners who started their own businesses and are now creating job opportunities for others as they get rich in the process.

• emotional cripples who have found and are enjoying a positive self-image. Destructive self-depreciation has been replaced by a healthy self-esteem, plus joy, hope, and love.

• troubled persons who suffered from frustrating, fractured relationships in love and marriage and who are now sailing on calm and sunny seas of life.

• physically handicapped persons and those in ill health, often facing death, who found that the stress that had been mountains to them was now gold mines. Scars turned into stars when possibility thinking took over.

Remember:

• Ideas have created great fortunes.

• Concepts have invented new products.

• Projects have grown into fantastic developments.

• Research and development have resulted in new enterprises by people who dared to believe in the Peak to Peek Principle of possibility thinking.

If you are one of the hundreds of thousands of readers or one of the millions of listeners and friends who have already learned the key to success, then welcome to this postgraduate course in supersuccessful living. You'll be thrilled to know that your greatest success will be your next effort. For you'll discover a universal, spiritual law—a cosmic mental principle called the Peak to Peek Principle.

Or if you are just joining the search for a better life, welcome aboard.

Now It's Your Turn

chapter one

Facing Life's Challenges

ARE YOU REALLY SATISFIED WITH YOUR LIFE as it is today?

If you are, you're in trouble. For to be totally content is to have no unfulfilled dreams. And when you stop dreaming, you start dying.

"Woe to those who are at ease in Zion."

Read on and experience challenging and glorious unrest again. Lift your eyes and see the unscaled mountains.

It takes guts to leave the ruts.

If you are not satisfied—and deeply sense there is something more you must do in your one life on earth—then join the expedition. I'm preparing to leave on an exciting venture—and you're invited to come along.

Whatever stage in life you're at today, you need to make a decision. You have four choices:

(1) Quit. Throw in the towel. Give up. Cash in. Abandon ship. Call it finished. Wait to die.

(2) Retreat. Back off. Step down. Retrench. Regroup. Cut back. Take it easy. Plan an early retirement.

(3) Shift into neutral. Take a reflective break. Review the whole situation. Plan a holiday. Stop racing. Let the competition pass you by. Seek solitude—and reevaluate your whole life.

(4) Move ahead deliberately, carefully, but boldly. Look up. Seek out paths that will promise a higher climb, with new vistas to surpass and transcend anything you've yet experienced.

So you have a decision you must make. Remember, even indecision is a decision.

But decision making is easy if your value system has not been clouded by internal contradictions.

What do you really want? The great psychiatrists have asked that question and have come up with different answers: "the will to pleasure" (Freud); "the will to power" (Adler); "the will to meaning" (Frankel). These are major theories that seek to answer your heart's deepest desire.

We have suggested in earlier books that all of the above theories are, to some degree during certain phases of life, valid analyses of basic human drives. But at the deepest level, the Will to Self-esteem is every person's Ultimate need and hunger. If, therefore, there is a contradiction in your value system among pleasure, power, meaning, or self-esteem, then choose the path to rising self-dignity!

That way you will strive for success. For success builds self-respect in yourself—even as failure threatens self-esteem. Ask the discouraged professor, the failing student, the divorced parents, the aging nonachiever, and see how damaging to the personality a sense of failure can be. You'll cringe when you see how the nonself-respecting person projects his insecurities on the world around him. Obviously, success is a noble objective!

The truth is that success is an unselfish goal, while failure is a selfish goal. It is impossible to succeed without helping a lot of people along the way. The secret of success is simple: find a hurt and heal it; find a problem and solve it; find an obstacle and remove it, bridge it, or turn it into an opportunity!

No business person can succeed unless he markets and manages his product or service according to this "find a need and fill it" principle. He sets his goals not based on his ego or financial needs, not by company policy or traditions, but by a careful reading of the human problems that generate authentic market pressures.

Yes, it's impossible to succeed without helping a lot of people along the way. And the opposite is also true:

You can fail, and you will fail, if you do not meet the needs of other persons.

And who fails when we fail? If the teacher, the religious leader, the parent, or the business person fails, who really fails? Who really gets hurt? Dozens, hundreds, perhaps thousands of innocent people whose needs will not be met. *They* are the real losers.

Therefore, there can be no room in our value systems for failure as a goal. There can be no substitute for success. Failure is not an option for the person who treasures his self-respect and really cares about other persons.

This book will show you how you can succeed by using what I call the Peak to Peek Principle. I guarantee it will work.

You will succeed even if you feel weak and ineffective. Your weakness will be replaced by an emerging self-confidence as you start to score personal successes.

You must soar before you can score. I know. This book will lift your thoughts. And you will begin to win.

With each successful experience you will gain inner power to climb higher. Success is a study of the flow of power: how to get it; how to keep it; how to share it; how to restrain it; how to use it; and when.

That's the life that can be your future if you will only believe, apply, and live by this powerful Peak to Peek Principle of successful living.

I'm not saying success is easy. The unselfish path never is. But it is enormously satisfying when you see how many people are helped along the way.

Dare to start a new way of life—here and now. Have you got courage? You'll need it.

You've got to soar before you can score!

Let's go and climb a mountain together!

chapter two

A Vital Force:
the Peak to Peek Principle

HAVE YOU NOTICED HOW SOME PEOPLE'S LIVES seem to be one success unfolding upon another? Each new achievement appears to upstage the previous one. Every new achievement seems to one-up the last success. That's the incredible way these lives unfold. The base gets bigger and the foundation seems to expand. Their achievement level continues to escalate and climb. How does one explain it?

Knowingly or unknowingly, these persons have tapped into a vital force I call the Peak to Peek Principle.

The question could be raised, "What comes first, achievement followed by a new vision or the vision followed by achievement?" I believe that the supersuccessful people have discovered a peak experience that gives them the vision of greater things they can accomplish.

What do I mean by a peak experience? A peak experience is a positive experience that affirms who you are and leaves you with an awareness that you are more than you ever thought you were. You succeed at something that may seem small to others but is a mountain scaled in your mind. It becomes a self-congratulatory experience that reveals present worth and, in the process, releases an early glimpse of your undeveloped potential. You begin to believe in great possibilities for your-

4

self. You are born again as you become a possibility thinker.

Michael Nason, the producer of the "Hour of Power," has a young daughter named Tara. He has told her story in the book *Tara*. Tara suffered from a brain injury at birth which left her without the capacity to walk. In fact, it left her deaf, dumb, and blind. It looked like she would be a vegetable all her life. Some eight years later she can see, she can hear, she can speak perfectly, but she cannot walk.

I recall the time her dad phoned with exciting news. For the first time Tara got on her hands and knees and had begun to creep. He said, "She held herself up for about thirty seconds on her own, on her hands and knees." Tara experienced a new vertical dimension as she raised her head to see things from a perspective she had never known before. This "peak" experience was a "peek" experience for Tara.

There are students of child development who contend that if a child skips the creep stage and goes from the crawl to the walk stage, he or she will have problems when the time to learn is reached. There's been a good deal of scientific research done to substantiate that theory. Creeping is very important to teach children coordination and perspective in learning, especially as it relates to understanding symbols encountered in reading.

Creeping is a peak experience! Later, when the child stands on two feet and takes the first few faltering steps and succeeds, this becomes a still greater peak experience. These peak experiences work miracles in the developing mind. They affirm to the child that "I am more than I ever realized I was." It's a positive experience, one that generates self-confidence. And every mountaintop experience becomes a vision-beholding experience. It tells me that *I can*. And the *I can* always leads to an exciting new *maybe*. The peak experience becomes a peek experience.

The tragedy is that there are some people who have never had a significant peak experience since they learned to walk.

A psychologist and I were talking about a person we were both trying to help. This person's whole life seemingly consisted of one failure after another. Each failure reinforced past failures in his mind and assured him that he would surely fail in any future undertaking as well. Some would call him a born loser.

The psychologist and I agreed. The trouble was that this person had never had a meaningful, that is, self-esteem-building, success experience. He squeezed through school. He suffered disappointments in relationships. He had no self-worth-affirming achievements. He failed in his first job, got fired from his second, and landed in a reform school. He lacked peak experiences. His last peak experience was when he learned to walk. The big onrush of positive emotion, the self-confidence-expanding emotional high present in his personal history occurred in childhood, when he learned to stand, walk, and run on his own two feet.

Many people become what we call failure-trapped in their mental attitude. They're afflicted with the "I can't do it" or "it won't work" syndrome. They go through life making excuses for avoiding opportunities. Think of that: deliberately making excuses for avoiding opportunities!

I read about a lady who, realizing that the New Year was quickly approaching, gloomily declared, "Go away tomorrow." That's sad, isn't it? I say, "Welcome tomorrow, for every new day creates a new opportunity to attempt to achieve a new peak experience."

Do you need a new success? Has it been a long time since you have had a mountaintop experience? Then you need a fresh emotional high, a new peak experience.

If life is stale, dull, or depressing in spite of past peak experiences and many personal successes, then you need a renewing self-esteem boost. After all, the self-esteem generated by a success experience has a limited life-span. So, at every age you need a new *peak* experience to give you a *peek* experience, a new vision of what you can be and a new consciousness of what you can do. You envision that what you can be far exceeds anything you've ever been before.

It's not until you climb the mountain that you see the great valley beyond that can be occupied and planted fruitfully. And that's why a person who has a meaningful peak experience obtains a greater vision. He catches the greater vision and reaches for a new peak. From the new peak he sees greater possibilities!

How can you have a peak experience?

You can begin by dreaming a greater dream. The dream gives rise to desire, the desire gives rise to the daring-to-do, the daring-to-do gives rise to the deciding-to-begin, and the deciding-to-begin gives rise to the deciding-to-try *seriously*.

Some of you may be afraid to begin. You don't think you can finish. You think, "Can I make it all the way to the top?"

Here's a great concept: Decide to begin and then decide to keep going. Don't worry about the top. Just decide to start and *keep going until you are past the point of no return*.

For ten years I have been a confirmed, dedicated, practicing jogger. One day, as I prepared to run, I realized I wasn't in the mood for running my customary four miles. My home is six miles from my office, so I got into my running suit and decided, "I'm only going to run just a little more than halfway from the house to the office." When I was a little more than halfway from the house to the office, what could I do? *It would then be easier to finish than to turn back*. In that way I finished a six-mile run.

I use this technique a lot in my life. When I know there is something that I should do but can't get up the drive, I only make the commitment to go as far as the point of no return. Then I'm trapped and I have to complete the job. The key is in deciding-to-begin.

One cannot ignore the most important ingredient in the Peak to Peek Principle of success. More important than culture, connections, or lucky breaks is the ingredient of belief.

Begin by believing in your own abilities to accomplish a higher goal for yourself than you ever have before. More than two thousand years ago a leader confidently and boldly affirmed, "Tomorrow I will stand at the top of the mountain!" He discovered the secret of the Peak to Peek Principle. He had a dynamic faith in himself, a positive faith in tomorrow.

The doubter never climbs mountains. His punishment is that he never enjoys the view from the mountaintop. His mind is never excited and enthused with bigger ideas, loftier dreams, and nobler visions!

"Tomorrow I will stand at the top of the mountain!" From the peak you will enjoy a peek into the new tomorrow. Your success cycle will have begun. From peak to peek. That's the secret.

chapter three

How the Peak to Peek Principle Works

THE PEAK TO PEEK PRINCIPLE FOR PROSPERITY: You have used it successfully, unless you were brain damaged (like Tara Nason) or born without legs. Chances are you have used the Peak to Peek Principle. You stood on two feet; saw farther; physically your eyes saw more. And an inrush of self-confidence resulted. You took that first faltering step, climbed up by holding onto a table or chair, tried again, fell once or twice, and kept at it until you were able to walk across the room. That achievement established a new vision. The "I did it" inspired a new "I can do it" so you set your mind on higher goals: to walk faster, then run, and finally jump.

My fourteen-year-old daughter, Carol, has had to learn to walk again—and hopefully will run and perhaps jump. She used the Peak to Peek Principle. When she was thirteen she was a passenger on a motorcycle that collided head on with a car. An hour later her left leg was being amputated in a Sioux City, Iowa, hospital, while her anguishing parents—half a world away in Korea—waited to board a plane to be at her side. It would be eight months, six surgical operations, and hundreds of IVs (intravenous injections) later before she would have her first artificial leg attached. Months later she and her dad would practice in the backyard. She would practice pitching a softball while standing without crutches. I shall never forget the painful sight of

9

watching her lay the crutches down and try—falteringly
—to take a step without them. I will long remember
seeing her try to move on to play the first-base position
in her school's girls softball game. I shall long remember the day she came home from her regular trips for
therapy. She was so enthused. "Dad," she exclaimed,
"I balanced for a whole minute while standing on my
leg—on my fake leg!" This was a peak experience that
released new hopes, new dreams, new visions, and new
beliefs, a peek into the future that could be hers if she
was willing to keep climbing.

By the time this book appears in print, I believe
she'll be running again. She quoted the popular slogans
I'd shared with millions of Americans via my books and
television programs. "Inch by inch, anything's a cinch."
"There is no gain without pain." "I've got to look at
what I have left, not at what I've lost." My daughter,
Carol, is climbing her peak. And she's getting a new
vision of what she can accomplish.

I saw this principle work in her darkest hour of
suffering. It was a torturous twenty-two-hour flight from
Korea to the Iowa hospital for Mrs. Schuller and me.

What would I say to my thirteen-year-old, I won-
dered as I cried.

My critics have often labeled my possibility philosophy as a shallow Pollyanna approach to life. Unknown
to me, Carol was using the Peak to Peek Principle
which accompanies possibility thinking. Here's how she
did it. Accompanying her in the sixty-minute ambulance ride from the scene of the accident was Dr.
Reuben Samoni of Sioux City, Iowa. Later he would
draw me aside and, with tear-filled eyes, say, "Dr.
Schuller, Carol is a brave and inspiring girl to me: She
fought bravely. You know, we gave her seventeen units
of blood. When we had her in surgery, we almost lost
her—we couldn't get a pressure reading or a pulse—
but we kept transfusing her and the pressure came back
up. What a fighter!

"As we were rushing her to the hospital," Dr. Samoni
continued, "she said to me during the hour-long, torturous ride, 'Can't you give me a shot for the pain,

doctor?' And I said, 'No, Carol. You've lost too much blood. Your pressure is too low.' She was quiet. Then she finally said, 'Doctor, I think I have to help people in life who are suffering. That's the reason I have to suffer. So I can help others who will have to suffer.' " *She had climbed her mountain of pain and had caught a vision of how her hurt could be turned into a halo.* The Peak to Peek Principle worked wonders!

Hours later my tired body stepped slowly, silently, tremblingly into the doorway of her private cubicle in the intensive care unit of St. Joseph's Hospital. I saw her lying there, white-faced, with her amputated stump hanging high in traction. Gone was her pretty ankle. Gone was her lovely leg. Her hair, arranged in two short ponytails, lay flat on the pillow on each side of her unmarred face. Her eyes opened wide. She saw me standing there with her mom at my side. Before either of us could utter a word, she broke the painful silence with a voice as calm as an airline pilot giving instructions to his crew.

"Dad, I think I know why it happened." Forcing back the tears, I replied, "Why, Carol?" And she replied firmly, confidently, "I think God has a special ministry for my life. To help people who've been hurt like I've been hurt. Like you always say, Dad, *'turn your scars into stars.'* "

In the weeks that followed she would receive telephone calls and telegrams from friends like John Wayne, Frank Sinatra, President Jimmy Carter, and Senator Ted Kennedy. But no letter meant more than a handwritten note received eight months later from Iowa. It was from Dr. Samoni, who had been with her in the ambulance. He would be credited with saving her life. Now, nearly a year later, he wrote, "I will always remember what an inspiration you were to me, Carol, when you said you were suffering so you could help ease the sufferings of others. I want to help you in whatever way you will choose to train yourself to do your life work. Enclosed is a check. Please let me be a small part of your good life." The check was almost exactly equal to the remuneration he received for his seven hours of uninterrupted lifesaving service.

Face your mountains and you'll gain a grand, new perspective of what you can do and be! The Peak to Peek Principle. Here's how it worked for a cab driver I met in New York City. He recognized my face, stopped the cab, jumped out, and asked for my autograph. I never did get his name, but I got his story.

"Dr. Schuller, I owe my life to your possibility thinking. I was unemployed. Never did have a job. Was a school dropout. I listened to you on TV in New York. I'm black—I live in a tough neighborhood. Then I heard you say, 'You can go anywhere from where you are.' I'll never forget that. I didn't agree. I yelled back at you. But my wife said, 'That's your trouble, man. You're an impossibility thinker. If you only listened—and believed—you could go anywhere you'd want to!' And I got into a fight with her. 'No one will hire me. I'm ignorant. I'm black,' I said, adding, 'Look at how many people are unemployed! There's nothing I can do.' She said, 'Not true. You can drive a car. Why not drive a taxi?' Dr. Schuller, I called the cab company and got this job. In one year I saved enough money to make a down payment on my own car." And as the driver explained in his own words, "The bank told me the other day, 'Hey, man, you're doing okay. Want to buy another car—and have a driver? We'll finance you. You've got good credit with us.' " Now he is on his way to building up his own fleet of cars. He has a successful business going—and, with it, self-esteem. He's latched onto the Peak to Peek Principle.

Here's how it worked for Jim Poppen. His cousin, Henry Poppen, who was on my staff, once told me, "You know, Jim wasn't a very special student when he went to Hope Academy in Holland, Michigan." I listened, for I graduated from the sister graduate school, Hope College. He continued, "But Jim went for one semester to Northwestern University, in Chicago, and during his first vacation his father found him on the kitchen floor in the middle of the night, tying strings around the legs of the chair. 'Don't bother me, Dad. I discovered the human brain in school. I want to be a brain surgeon and I have to learn to tie knots in the dark. I'm practicing.' " So he got a peek, a glimpse, a vision of a dream! Of a mountain to climb. A peek of a peak. His first peak was college. He made it. His second peak was medical school. He passed!

Years later, when he died, the Manchester, New Hampshire, *Union Leader* featured his life in the following front-page editorial written by the publisher, William Loeb:

HE WALKED WITH KINGS
BUT NEVER LOST THE
COMMON TOUCH

The world's greatest neurosurgeon, Dr. James Poppen, who died last weekend, had a number of patients in New Hampshire. More importantly, because his life was an illustration of how to be the best in your field, but never let it go to your head, this newspaper feels his passing requires comment.

In 1968, on the night Bobby Kennedy was shot, in the middle of that night the phone alongside Dr. Poppen's bed in Brookline, Massachusetts, rang. A Texas voice on the other end said, "Dr. Poppen, this is President Johnson. We have a supersonic jet waiting at the airport. Will you get there as fast as you can to fly out to California and see what you can do for Bobby Kennedy?"

When Aristotle Onassis's only son had a severe head injury, as a result of an airplane accident in Greece, Aristotle and Jackie Kennedy Onassis and Dr. Poppen, the three of them alone in a jet, raced to Greece to see what could be done. But, again, the damage was so extensive that no medical genius could save the boy.

All over the world, premiers, ministers of finance and world figures such as the late President of Argentina Peron were Dr. Poppen's patients—because he was known as the greatest and the best in his field.

That sort of success might very well have gone to any

man's head, but the remarkable thing about Jim Poppen was that he never lost a sense of awe in dealing with every human being whose medical problems he confronted. He was as much interested in the humblest of patients as he was in the greatest.

Just a year or two ago, this writer wanted to reach him on the telephone for some advice, and located him and talked to him, finally, in Bogota, Colombia. The altitude there is about 12,000 feet and even for a younger person that altitude is difficult to handle.

In replying to the question of what he was doing there, he said, "Well, there are some people I know here who have some problems. They can't afford the cost of the high-priced rooms in Boston, so I am operating here."

Those fortunate patients who came under his care noted not only his technical skill, but also his understanding of all sorts of people. His way of handling them was really almost as much of a miracle to watch as his operating technique.

Of his technique, a visiting foreign surgeon once said to Dr. Charles Fager, who succeeded Dr. Poppen as head of the Neurosurgery Department at the Lahey Clinic, "It's amazing; here is this huge bear of a man (he was a great baseball player in his youth who earned money to go to medical school by playing with the old Baltimore Orioles), and yet when I watch his hands in the operating room, it is like watching a ballet dancer."

Dr. Fager said, "I never dared tell Dr. Poppen that remark because he did not appreciate flattery."

The best comment, of course, on what Dr. Poppen meant to the world of his day could be seen in the nature of the throng that filled the New England Baptist Hospital Memorial Chapel. There were the great who could be recognized from the pages of any newspaper, but there were also the little people whom he had helped, white and black, and there were the operating nurses, who came right from the operating room and still wore their gowns and caps to cover their hair.

They were all paying tribute to a man who proved that it is still possible in this age of synthetic, well-publicized bogus heroes for a man to be truly a great man and yet to conduct himself with modesty.

The fact that Dr. Poppen's professional services were in demand from people all over the world never caused him to be anything but unaffected, always with an open mind to new ideas and always eager to help a patient, no matter how unimportant that individual might be as the world saw him or her.

Those who knew Jim Poppen, as this writer did, and who were the beneficiaries of his skill, know that we will not see his like again.

The Peak to Peek Principle is the surest way to successful self-esteem. To repeat, it's not easy. Mountain climbing isn't for softies or babies.

THE *TASSEL* IS
WORTH THE HASSLE

My son, Robert junior, had just received his diploma. Four years of hard college studies had now brought him to a new peak experience. He held his black mortarboard cap in his hand, fingering the long black silk tassel. We looked proudly into each other's eyes. "It's a great feeling," he said, adding, "It was hard work, but it's worth it." "You're so right, Bob," I replied. "Year after year you'll know the tassel is worth the hassle."

If you use your successful education as a means of turning your life into a greater service to God and your fellow humans, you'll realize that the rewards are worth the effort. A successful experience becomes a self-esteem or peak experience when it allows you to become more helpful to troubled people who need help.

If, however, you look for ego-boosting, recognition, awards, plaudits, and honor outside the arena of unselfish service, you'll never get enough. And you'll be convinced that the tassel wasn't worth the hassle. But if you look back on the people whom you've been able to help because you chose to be a success, then, truly, you'll have that wonderful feeling of self-esteem and you'll say, "It was worth it. It really was! I'd do it all over again even if I knew how tough the path would be, how costly the trip, and how painful the climb. The peak has given me a peek into how wonderful one life can really become when we give our dream all we've got."

The Peak to Peek Principle. Here's how I've used it in my work. This book is being published on the twenty-fifth anniversary of the founding of the church I serve, which I started with my wife, my oldest daughter, my young son, and only five hundred dollars. I began with a dream. It gave me a glimpse, a vision, a peek into the future. I "saw" myself starting from point zero and adding members committed to meeting the emotional needs of nonreligious people.

We knew no one and had no contacts. So we spent a few dollars putting ads in the paper encouraging people to attend our first worship service in a drive-in theater.

Of the five hundred dollars we had, I spent three hundred dollars in the lumberyard alone. I made a crude cross with my own saw, hammer, and nails, and put it on the roof of the snack bar that served as a worship center. And I spent a few dollars for an old wooden chair that I could sit in and for some plywood for a makeshift pulpit.

My first "peak" was 150 members. We reached that goal in six months. The drive-in ministry succeeded, and before long our first little church on two acres of land became a reality, complete with pews, carpet, and a simple organ. It was beautiful! Then we reached another "peak."

As we grew and filled the church with happy people, our vision expanded. The peak experience produced a fresh peek experience. Five years later we moved into a larger building that could seat one thousand persons, built at a cost of nearly one million dollars. Our membership now was over the one thousand mark. We had reached a new peak and, in the process, found ourselves stronger in human, financial, and spiritual resources than we'd ever experienced before. We were strong enough now to think bigger than ever. By the time we celebrated our fifteenth anniversary, we had six thousand members and our "large" church had "enlarged" and expanded to seat nearly two thousand persons. We had reached a new peak, which released within us an awareness of how our power base had really solidified and expanded. This inspired us to think bigger than ever. The higher peak gave us a loftier peak! We were strong enough now to envision televising our church services each Sunday in Los Angeles! This would cost four hundred thousand dollars a year, but we had the membership base to contemplate that new development with financial responsibility. Our new peak projected a new peek of a higher peak! So, to celebrate our fifteenth birthday we televised our service on one station in Los Angeles. When it succeeded, we dreamed of expanded service to more cities. And two years later we were televising our program in Chicago, Philadelphia, New York, Los Angeles, and Seattle! Each new peak gave us greater confidence. Slowly, solidly, we expanded as we gained the strength to expand *without* borrowing money. The broader the base grew, the greater our strength felt, the greater our vision expanded. Each new peak released a new peek of new peaks to scale. With the publication of this book, our church membership will have exceeded the ten thousand mark. (It is the largest church in the oldest Protestant denomination with a continuous ministry in the United States. The Reformed Church in America, which started in 1628 with fifty-nine Dutch colonists, all of whom belonged to the Reformed Church in Holland. Among other churches, they founded what continues as the Marble Collegiate Church in New York City, made famous in this century by its celebrated pastor, Norman Vincent Peale.) The television program is aired on over 150 stations in the United States. (That's the size of each of the major U.S. networks— CBS, ABC, and NBC.) It's also aired in Australia, Canada, and over the Armed Forces networks.

To accommodate the overflow crowds, we shall, on our twenty-fifth anniversary, dedicate our "ultimate church home"—the three-thousand-seat Crystal Cathedral—to serve our larger membership and to meet the vastly expanded needs of a worldwide ministry. A new peak is about to be scaled. As I write these words, the advance climbers in our expedition have reached the summit and have raised the flag.

By the time you read these words, we shall have reached the peak. The Crystal Cathedral will have been dedicated, debt-free, to the glory of God and the service of the community. Our twenty-fifth anniversary will find us on our own property, valued at well over twenty-five million dollars—mortgage free. That's success! That's power! "Or what?" you ask. What "peeks" will we get when we stand on that all-time high peak of a Crystal Cathedral? The answer is that we'll use our expanded power to reach further and do more good for more hurting people than we'd ever dreamed was possible when we started.

Even as I write this, I'm planning to use our power base as a launching pad to establish "Good Samaritan Inns" around the world. We are also planning a million-dollar emergency-relief medical center in a remote jungle region of Mexico, with roads, ambulances, and a landing strip. We are envisioning getting a mental peek and dreaming of collecting that million dollars in one year's time, following the dedication of the Crystal Cathedral.

The Peak to Peek Principle—it's absolutely mountain-moving, miracle-working! Read on and you'll see how this principle works and how you can make it work for you.

chapter four

Getting Mentally Acclimated for High Altitudes

WHERE DO YOU BEGIN?

"I've got to see it before I believe it!" the negative thinker announced. I corrected him. "You've got to believe it before you'll see it! *You have to think before you'll blink. The dream precedes the scheme.*"

Your thinking must rise to envision possibilities before you'll even try for higher achievements.

Begin with what you have. Bloom where you are planted. Start with the positive thinking power of thanksgiving. Count your blessings. Add up all of your assets. The altitude begins with the attitude of gratitude. For my daughter, Carol, it meant thanking God that her brain was not injured; thanking God that she still could *see* and *hear* and *think* and *talk;* and thanking God that she still had one leg and two hands and possessed the freedom, so valued in the United States, to pick any goals she wanted to!

The Peak to Peek Principle starts with the *attitude* of *gratitude*, which releases get-going, start-growing, and keep-glowing powers.

Let me share with you the six powers, available to us in our Peak to Peek experiences, which are released by the attitude of gratitude.

I. SURVIVING POWER

The attitude of gratitude releases *surviving power*. "I'm grateful I'm alive," my daughter Carol said after her leg was amputated. The energy to hang in and not give up on your future is the first power you need. The attitude of gratitude gives you surviving power, which means you will not quit.

I was born and raised on an Iowa farm. I vividly remember the dust bowl years. When I was a child, in the thirties, the wind swept in from the Dakotas. It was dry, dusty, violent, and fierce. The wind became our enemy because it would peel off the dry, rich, black soil and swirl it like drifting dunes in the gullies and canyons of our fields. I shall never forget one particularly difficult year. We walked around our farm with white towels over our faces to keep from suffocating in the choking dust.

Then the harvest season came. My father would normally harvest a hundred wagonfuls of corn, but that year he harvested not the usual one hundred loads but a meager half wagonload. I can still see the old wagon standing in the yard—only half full. It was a total crop failure, one that has never been equaled.

I shall never forget how, seated at the dinner table with his calloused hands holding ours, my father looked up and thanked God. He said, "I thank you, God, that I have *lost nothing*. For I have regained the seed I planted in the springtime." He used half a wagonload for seed; he got half a wagonload back.

His attitude of gratitude was that he had lost nothing while other farmers were complaining that they had lost ninety loads or one hundred loads. *They counted their losses by what they hoped they could have harvested.*

I'll always remember my father saying, "You can never count up the might-have-beens or you will be defeated." Never look at what you have lost; look at what you have left. Those words of wisdom from my father, whose education stopped at the sixth grade, were of immeasurable value in making me the possibility thinker that I am today.

The attitude of gratitude gave my father surviving power. He went right back and planted that seed the next year. When he finally retired, he was no longer a poor farmer. With his attitude of gratitude he prayed, planned, plugged along, and prospered, leaving a nice estate for his children.

The attitude of gratitude provides surviving power— you don't quit when you're counting your blessings. In turn, this thanksgiving thinking begins to release other powers to help you set new goals, make bold decisions, and move forward confidently to solve problems.

II. REVIVING POWER

The second power that the attitude of gratitude releases is *reviving power*. The attitude of gratitude not only helps you survive, it also provides reviving power. You find the power to start again when you feel like quitting, to pick up the pieces and bounce back for a comeback.

Stop and think for a moment. What have been your little successes? Your victories? Some of you may be in a hospital. *You've got to count your blessings.* Perhaps you can't walk yet, but you can move your arms. You can't get out and do some things, but you can do things that you couldn't do at other times. Count your peak experiences! Add them up. Concentrate on them. Look at the positive aspects.

Not all peak experiences become peek experiences that lead to a greater vision. That only happens if the attitude of gratitude permeates the success experience.

There are persons who have their successes, or peak experiences, but instead of being motivated to move out and accomplish more, they reach the top of their mountain and complain because they didn't do better. Or they complain because they didn't climb faster. Or they compare their accomplishment to someone who seemingly has surpassed their achievement, and instead of rejoicing in their success they become depressed. Their peak experience is turned into a valley experience because they have a negative, nongrateful attitude.

The peak experience should give us grateful visions of greater accomplishments, where achievement gives rise to greater vision, greater vision gives rise to greater belief, and greater belief gives rise to greater confidence. One peak leads to a new peek into what greater things we can do.

We define a peak experience as an experience that leaves you with a self-affirming awareness that you are more than you ever thought you were. It is this positive attitude that turns a peak experience into a vision-expanding peek experience.

Begin by saying "thank you" to the persons who live with you and work with you. Each day mention a specific quality of work or attitude they display that is helpful to you. Let others know how much you appreciate them. Carry a diary of gratitude with you everywhere you go and record all the nice experiences that happen, the nice people you meet. It is amazing to contemplate the powers you will unlock and release within yourself with this discipline. The attitude of gratitude begins each day with the feeling, "thank God for letting me live today" and each new day begins anew with a peak to peek experience.

To really come alive you need (1) surviving power and (2) reviving power. And now, as you keep on keeping on affirming gratitude, you will feel the onrush of *striving power*.

III. STRIVING POWER

Because I am grateful, I have a new enthusiasm that helps me to strive, set new goals, make additional decisions, and solve problems. The positive mental attitude of gratitude taps and releases an initial enthusiasm which can get you started! That's often the hardest job.

Instead of bemoaning your lot, complaining about your shortcomings, start adding up your assets and your opportunities and a new experience of gratitude will release the energy to try. You strive in three areas: (a) in goal setting; (b) in decision making; and (c) in problem solving. That's how the striving power will turn your peak experience into a new peek experience. You'll get the motivation to set goals, make decisions, and solve problems. *That comes through striving power!*

IV. DIVING POWER

The attitude of gratitude that produces striving power will then release *diving power*. The power to dive in and start a new venture. Remember Mark Spitz? After he broke several records in the Olympics, he was exhausted. By the time he picked up his last gold medal, he was so tired that he announced he was going to quit swimming. His peak experience, instead of becoming a peek experience, became a bleak experience. With the attitude of gratitude the peak experience gives you the power to dive in again and set new goals. With diving power the peak experience can and will be a peek experience. The alternative is not retirement but the beginning of a slow death.

Observing a professional tree surgeon who was supervising the moving of trees, I asked him, "Will these trees grow any higher?" "They will as long as they live," he answered, adding, "As long as a tree is living, it is still growing." He explained, "People say to me 'This tree is full-grown.' But they're wrong. A tree only stops growing when it is dead." The same is true of persons, corporations, communities, and institutions. When there's life, there's growth.

V. DRIVING POWER

The attitude of gratitude turns a peak experience into a *driving power* experience. Enormous energy is released when a person counts his blessings. What happens when you start counting your blessings? You become positive. When you become positive you acquire enthusiasm. Enthusiasm is energy. Show me an enthusiastic person and I'll show you a person who's energetic, dynamic, and positive. When emotional energy is released, you have driving power.

I recall again how I saw the attitude of gratitude

release driving power in my father. It was the time a tornado dropped without warning like a slithering snake out of the black sky and wormed its way toward our farm house. We jumped into our car and escaped with our lives. But the black, serpentine cloud dropped its poisonous head and sucked up all our nine buildings. It left our farm totally destroyed! The night after the disaster a prayer meeting was held in a little country church, where I heard my father pray, "Oh God, I thank you that not a life was lost, not a human bone was broken. We have lost nothing that cannot be recaptured and regained. And through the storm we have kept everything that would have been irreplaceable—especially our faith."

That attitude of gratitude gave my father driving power. It gave him enthusiasm. We went to town and bought the remnants of an old four-story house that was, for many months, in the process of being dismantled—sold section by section the way a four-layer chocolate cake is sold by the slice. One last section still stood waiting to be bought for fifty dollars by someone who would be willing to remove it. So we bought it and began, carefully and tediously, to dismantle it nail by nail, board by board. We hauled each shingle and plank to the place where our farm had stood and began to rebuild a new home over the empty hole in the ground that was the basement of our previous house. When we focused on what we could do, rather than on what we had lost, we became grateful once more. And that released the energy to climb up and onward!

VI. ARRIVING POWER

The sixth power is *arriving power*. You make it! You succeed!

While you are focusing on the mountaintop experiences of your life, your emotions will be positive. You will be receptive to a bigger dream, a greater vision, a higher hope! The peak experience will truly become a peek experience. Out of the success will come a new dream, out of the new dream will come greater confidence, and you'll have a success cycle going that nothing can stop. So you arrive at the top with great qualities of character, humility, and unselfishness. Humility: the understanding that the team did it. You realize they tackled, they opened up the field, they took the bruises, they did the blocking. All you did was hold the ball and run.

That's the attitude of gratitude. Try it and you get surviving power, reviving power, striving power, diving power, driving power, and arriving power. In the process you become an authentically humble person while at the same time expanding your sense of self-esteem. You turn your peak experience into a peek experience. "I can do more than I ever thought I could before . . . but I couldn't do it alone." You affirm. No one climbs to the top of the mountain by himself.

And then you also arrive with unselfishness. Gratitude is nothing more than saying, "I am indebted." Gratitude is saying "thank you" to this person, to that friend, to your community, to your country, and to God.

It is impossible to become a vain, egotistical, selfish person if you maintain the attitude of gratitude. That's why truly successful people are always genuinely humble! By contrast, the failing person is (a) ungrateful, (b) selfish, and (c) headed for more failures! In his ingratitude he complains. And this complaining, ungrateful attitude feeds his self-pity and his self-serving, immature emotionalism. Such a person becomes more self-seeking, more self-possessing, and more self-serving. In the process, this person drives away the beautiful, positive people and ends up lonely—setting in motion a lifestyle grooved to fresh failures.

Are you a grateful person? Have you had a peak experience lately? A victory? An accomplishment? A high adventure? An experience that affirmed to you that you were better or bigger than you thought you were? If you haven't, today is the time to begin. Begin by thanking God for what you have. Legs? Eyes? Ears? Hands? A mind capable of dreaming daring dreams? Okay! You're on your way! Now pick a peak and start climbing!

chapter five

The Secret of Successful Mountain Climbing

ANYONE WHO WANTS TO SUCCEED can do so. Success can take many forms. It may be recovering from surgery or rebuilding your body after an accident. It may be starting a new life after a torturous experience of rejection and divorce. It may be pursuing a new career at the age of sixty-five. Whatever it is, you can succeed.

Believe in success. What do we mean by success? *Success is building self-esteem in yourself and others through sacrificial service to God and to your fellow human beings.* You may accumulate riches, fame, and honors, but unless you achieve tremendous self-esteem in the process, all that the world calls success becomes ashes in your hands.

The secret of success is to find a need and fill it.

S-U-C-C-E-S-S

S—Select your goal.

U—Unlock your negative thinking.

C—Chart your course.

C—Commit yourself.

E—Expect problems and difficulties.

S—Sacrifice yourself. (Yes, success always involves a cross!)

S—Stick with it. (You never fail until you say, "I quit.")

It all spells SUCCESS!

Believe that you can and will succeed! And sometimes, strangely and unexpectedly, you will find yourself at a moment when people will say, "He's got it made! *He has hit the heights!* He has arrived! He made it! He won!" Discover how universal and unchangeable the laws of success really are.

S—Select Your Goal

If you aim at nothing, you'll hit nothing. If your goals are vague, your achievements will be vague. But if your decisions are specific, you will harvest specific results. Select your goal. I can't believe the staggering number of people who go through life completely at the whim of forces to which they have surrendered their destiny! The vast majority of persons never assume leadership of their future. They live casually and loosely. They don't plan!

Then select the right goal. Have you heard of the company that developed a new dog food? All the necessary nutrients—protein, minerals, fats, and carbohydrates—were included in the product. The company came out with a brand-new package and a national advertising program which included full-page ads and ingenious commercials. Everything was planned and designed to be a success.

After six months of sales, which had started slowly, dwindled to nothing. The chairman of the board called all the district sales managers together in a major meeting in Chicago.

"What's wrong?" he asked. "Look at the beautiful full-page ads we have in national magazines. Look at the expensive commercials on television."

He held up a box of the dog food and pointed to the back of the box. He read the contents and admired the beautiful packaging. "The cost is even lower than our competitors," he added. "Now tell me why you people aren't selling this dog food?"

You could hear a pin drop. Then someone at the back of the room slowly came to his feet and said, "Sir, the dogs don't like it."

The secret of success cannot be found by sitting in an expensive leather chair in a plush office and dreaming your dreams. The secret of success is to select a goal by finding a need and filling it. Find a hurt and heal it. Find somebody with a problem; offer to help solve it.

S—Select your goal; then

U—Unlock your negative thinking.

I talked to a businessman who said, "I've failed, but it's not my fault." And do you know why he said that? Because he blamed his failure on everybody else. He attacked the unions, government regulations, the tax structure, and the competition. I had to say to him, in as friendly and yet as firm a manner as I could, "Sir, in the final analysis you threw in the towel, they didn't. You said, 'I give up.' You decided to quit." At that point he finally admitted, "I guess I did."

If you fail it is because you choose to fail. And there are reasons why many people choose to fail. The price is too high. Total commitment is too costly (you'll eliminate all other options and alternatives if you're totally committed), so the risk is too great. Your security or your freedom is threatened by total commitment. Remember, associates, family, friends, or enemies may create problems for you, but nobody but you can and will ever make the final decision to *quit*. And nobody has failed until he's decided to throw in the towel. Only you can choose to kill your dream. Nobody else can make that decision.

You must believe in success. After all, the alternative is to believe in failure. And God has not planned your life to be a failure. For when you fail, many other innocent persons will be hurt. So, to accept failure as a good is the ultimate selfish act.

Believe in success, for success means discovering God's beautiful plan for your life and allowing it to develop to its fullest potential.

God plans for success and believes in it!

S—Select your goal.

U—Unlock your negative thinking.

C—Chart your course.

You will start to succeed when you chart your way to the top of the mountain. Make a game plan. Imagine how your resources can be channeled, focused, controlled, and managed to achieve your loftier objectives. Develop a two-year plan, a five-year plan, and a ten-year plan. Think ahead!

S—Select your goal.

U—Unlock your negative thinking.

C—Chart your course.

C—Commit yourself.

Success doesn't just happen. It requires a genuine and sincere commitment. The greater the good, the higher the peak, the riskier the venture, the higher the price to be paid. So, great successes always call for a great sacrifice. The tragedy is, of course, that we are tempted to accept the lower road of human achievement. After all, it's easier and much less risk is involved. And there's more time for leisure. But at the end of the road there is no feeling as great as standing on a mountaintop, even if you are scared and bleeding and bruised. There is no feeling of satisfaction that can compare with carrying your cross, making your commitment, and doing what God wants you to do.

E—Expect problems and difficulties.

Every time God gives you His plan, it will appear to be impossible. However, it will be possible if you take one step forward. Take that one vital step; move as far as you can.

S—Sacrifice yourself.

Successful people are always conscious of their imperfections. No one is ever perfect. Frustrated? Ask what you may be doing wrong. Be ready to change your style if need be. "I'd rather be successful than have my own way," I tell my associates. "I'm not on an ego trip. I'm on a success trip," I often add, reminding myself and others that people who never change their minds are either perfect—or stubborn.

Carefully and prayerfully ask God's guidance. He gives me guidance and I believe He will for you. I say: "Lord, I think I'm getting your message. I think this is your plan for my life. But God, if I am reading the signal wrong, close the door. Block the way. Make it impossible for me to move ahead. And God, if I'm reading your signals right, open the door so I can take the next step forward." And if He keeps leading you on then never give up.

S—Stick with it.

Yes, successful mountain climbers have perseverance —if they have anything!

THE END OF THE ROAD
OR ONLY A BEND?

I remember when Mrs. Schuller, the children, and I came from the Midwest to California. We came across a mountain ridge and stopped to view the great valley beyond. The road stretched as straight as an arrow for as far as we could see. But as we came closer and closer to the mountain ridge, it looked like the road stopped dead. But we didn't stop and turn around; we kept on going. And, sure enough, twenty miles down that straight road we saw that the road gradually curved. And as we followed the curve, it became a pass through the mountains.

That's the way it is with success! You get started even though you see a huge mountain range that makes it impossible to see beyond. You just keep on going and at the right moment the end becomes a bend.

I can tell you what God's plan for your life is in general terms. This is a universal principle. God wants to use you to do something beautiful in the world around you. That's it in one sincere sentence. God created you and allowed you to be born because He wanted to use you where you are . . .

to find a hurt and heal it

to find somebody with a problem and help them solve it

to find someone who's trapped and help them discover liberty and freedom

to find someone who is defeated and lift him up again and give him new hope and a new dream.

So believe in success and choose to succeed. For you're bound to help someone along the way. It's impossible to succeed without being a servant to someone. So believe that you can succeed if you really want to!

chapter six

How to Handle Impossibilities

SELF-CONFIDENT AND SELF-AFFIRMING PERSONS are people who latch on to and hatch great possibilities by living out the Peak to Peek Principle. They are the ones who run to the mountains, welcome risk-taking adventures, and hit the heights.

It is on the mountain peaks that you gain the great reward—you get a glimpse into your genius. A vision of your greatness. A peek into the person you really are. So you gain life's great gift: self-confidence. Self-confidence is never taught, it must always be caught.

And there is no creativity apart from self-confidence. You cannot take a course in creative thinking. Self-confidence is learned not *in* a course but *on* a course! You can only learn it on the course when you get out there alone and face your challenges. For then you are the first to spot the tremendous opportunities waiting for those willing to take the risk.

While I was jogging one morning before daybreak, I thought to myself, "What a beautiful experience it is to run through the silence of the dying night and the about-to-be-born morning, to feel the blood surging through my system. What a tremendous sense of vitality."

As I was running, I looked up and saw the hills east of my home glowing in the sunlight. As I scanned the valley to the west, I saw the lingering shadows of the night lounging in the valley like giants that had outlasted their welcome but still did not know when to take their leave.

And that's when I had the revelation. "The tall trees caught the sunlight first!" The tips of the trees became golden and bright as the rising sun hit the pointed tops, while the branches that hung just above the ground were still dark under the lingering shadows of the night, which had not been fully dismissed. The sun's first rays hit the mountaintops before they reached into the valleys.

Peak people are the first people to peek. People who stand tall are the first ones to spot the opportunities. They have a different perspective. They are the first to catch the light of other opportunities. People who've latched on to the peak experiences in life are usually the first people to move ahead. They become super-achievers because they are those who are first in line to buy a theater ticket; they move into the territory when the price is still low; they spot the opportunity before anybody else; they see where the growing edge is going to be and they're ahead of the masses.

They have learned to rise to the top! From their peak they have not only the perspective to spot opportunities but also the perceptivity and discernment to see the undeveloped possibilities that lie beyond. They get a peek, or a vision, indicating where to move next. The Peak to Peek Principle.

Self-confident, self-affirmed, self-esteemed persons are those who have latched on to and hatched great possibilities by living out the Peak to Peek Principle. They have a different mental attitude toward impossible situations. The greatest reward they receive when they reach the top is something that cannot be taught in schools, universities, or in a collective experience: It is self-confidence. And self-confidence is what produces creative thinking.

After twenty-five years of studying, writing, teaching, and lecturing about possibility thinking, I have this to share with you: The single most distinctive quality that distinguishes the outstanding person from the mediocre person is the fact that *great people have a different mental attitude toward impossible situations*.

The exceptional person is an average person who has a distinctive attitude toward impossibilities. That explains why people who have peak experiences and rise to the top of the mountain oftentimes are not distinguished by their IQ or their Ph.D. as much as they are by their M.A. (mental attitude).

That's the key! Look at all the great people. The really great people have a different mental attitude toward mountains. It is their positive mental attitude toward impossible situations that, more than anything else, sets them apart from the low-achieving, low-confidence crowd. People who have peak experiences are those who tackle a great cause that appears to be impossible but is unquestionably honorable. And they do it in the name of God; in the name of their fellow human beings; in the name of their ancestors; and in the name of their unborn descendants. They turn impossibilities into possibilities and that is what sets them apart as great leaders and outstanding winners. They think tall, they stand tall, and they are the first to catch the sunrise of creative ideas!

Great people are average people with a different attitude toward impossible situations. What I want to share with you is incredibly simple. There are only three choices before you when you face an impossibility. Your first choice is to be *intimidated* by impossibilities. That's what happens to most people. Your second choice is to be *frustrated* by impossibilities. That's what happens to the losers. And your third choice is to be *motivated* by impossibilities. That's what happens to winners.

I. INTIMIDATED

How do you handle an impossibility? You are *intimidated* by an impossibility when (1) you do nothing because you fear failure; (2) you do nothing because you are afraid of criticism; (3) you do nothing because you are uncertain of success; (4) you do nothing because you're afraid of the cost; (5) you do nothing because you can't be sure of perfection; (6) you do nothing about this beautiful, impossible idea because you see something about it that's not right—there's something wrong with the best idea; (7) you do nothing because you're not sure you'd get credit for success if you managed to make it.

To be intimidated means that you come up against a mountain and say it's impossible to climb. The massive peak overpowers and silences you. So you withdraw, you give up, you're intimidated by the mountain.

I have been in committee meetings where someone has come up with a masterful, pace-setting, creativity-releasing, human-need filling, obstacle-busting, problem-solving, hurt-healing idea. Then someone else has come along and said, "We've got to leave quite soon. Can we have the treasurer's report?" That would kill the idea right there. Or else somebody might say, "It's impossible!" And *that word "impossible"* intimidates the group. Vast organizations, businesses, institutions, and corporations use threats and intimidation as a negative motivating force for employees. (Then they wonder why the basic output is so limited in relation to man-hours invested.) Impossibilities stop some people yet motivate others. Get turned on by an impossibility! Don't be intimidated by it!

Albert Einstein was once asked, "How did you discover relativity?" And his answer was, "I questioned and challenged an axiom."

Do you want to know the secret of success? Ask any greatly successful person and he will say, "I refused to be intimidated by an impossibility. I challenged the impossibility!" If impossibilities intimidate you, then you are a loser. To allow yourself to be intimidated means that you're defeated already.

II. FRUSTRATED

Another roadblock you face with a presumed impossibility is *frustration*. That means you're upset!

The difference between intimidation and frustration is quite clear. A person who's intimidated has been silenced. His voice has been cut off. He has been rendered neutral. That's damaging because it's so deadly. But a person who is frustrated is still alive. He wishes to God that the mountain would not be there. He wishes to God that the problem would go away. He's not defeated yet. He hasn't given up. He's alive enough to be frustrated, but he has a negative attitude toward the situation. And because he has a negative attitude he is finding that all his negative emotions are being charged up.

Here is a fundamental psychological and theological truth: Creativity does not happen in a tense environment. Tranquility is the mental climate in which creativity happens. And tension blocks the flow of creative ideas!

The terrible thing about frustration is that it tempts you to stop thinking positively. Frustration produces a willingness to yield to negative thoughts. This, in turn, produces tension, which constricts the potential flow of creative ideas. New, innovative, bright, pace-setting solutions are blocked!

I recall meeting the head of a South Korean command post while there on a visit. I was told why the colonel in the command position was so great. My informant said, "I'll give you an idea of what kind of a guy he is. He's a great possibility thinker. We faced an impossible situation a year ago and he called in his top engineers and his top assistants. There were about twelve of us. 'Look,' he said, 'we are faced with an impossible situation. But we all know that, so I don't want anybody reminding me. I want every ounce of mental power in this room to focus on solutions. Go back and dream up a solution.' Forty-eight hours later we collectively came up with a great idea. He motivated us and the impossibility was turned into a possibility!"

Don't be intimidated by an impossibility. Don't be frustrated by it. The only cure for not being frustrated is to look upon it as an opportunity, not as an obstacle. You will be motivated!

III. MOTIVATED

Choose to be *motivated*, motivated enough to call smarter people, motivated enough to be able to listen to other key people. I'm thinking of a business executive who wouldn't listen to his advisers because he was afraid that if he followed their advice they'd get all the credit and he wouldn't receive a promotion. The end result was that nobody came up with solutions to various problems and there was no credit for anyone. The whole ship sank and he was on the ship.

If there is a seemingly impossible situation in an interpersonal relationship between you and another person, be motivated to ask yourself the extent to which you caused the situation to develop.

An interesting thing happened to me one morning on the way to my office. I was driving an old car that I had bought seven years earlier. It's been such a faithful old car. A few miles from our church I looked at the speedometer and watched the little odometer blocks change: 99,999.5 . . . 99,999.6 . . . 99,999.7 . . . 99,999.8 . . . 99,999 9. Then it read 00,000.0. I had a brand-new car! It sat in the parking lot all day with only three miles on it.

Now we all know that you cannot tell the newness of a car by the mileage gauge, just as you can't tell a book by its cover. It's not a new car just because the gauge reads 00,000.0. That car can't be re-created into a brand-new car, but you can be re-created into a brand-new person!

You become a new person when you learn one of life's most important lessons: Every problem is a possibility in disguise. Every impossibility is a fantastic opportunity, an opportunity to:

1. start a business
2. improve your business
3. start a new career
4. start a new relationship
5. repair a neglected relationship
6. invent a new product

7. grow personally
8. learn your faults, things that your ego has long blinded you from seeing, or
9. be alone to reflect, meditate, and think things through or? . . . or? . . . or?

Whatever you do, remember: Nothing new happens until some creative person tackles an impossible situation! Today's impossibilities are tomorrow's breakthroughs. Progress never starts until someone challenges a long-standing impossibility. Climbing a mountain? Trying to reach your peak? Facing an impossibility? Good! God is just trying to motivate you. You haven't begun to discover your real strength.

chapter seven

Three Paths to the Peak

LET ME REMIND YOU AGAIN what I mean by the Peak to Peek Principle. A peak experience is an experience of success, achievement, and accomplishment which feeds your self-esteem. The *peak* experience gives you a *peek* experience—a vision of greater accomplishments that you can realize if you will (1) believe, (2) begin, (3) beware of negative thinking, and (4) be sure of ultimate success.

Without the mountaintop experience you'll never have the visionary experience. Without a successful experience of personal achievement you'll lack the belief in yourself to see the greater possibilities that still lie untapped within you. You and I need the peak experience before we will ever have a peek experience.

There are three paths that people try to take to the top of the mountain, three attitudes you can take toward success. I can sum them up in three simple words that contain vital principles for living. I call the first path the *toss* approach, the second path the *boss* approach, and the third path the *cross* approach.

I. TOSS

First, there's the *toss* approach. Some people have a flippant attitude toward life: no plans, no goals, no commitments. Would anybody flip a coin to see which

39

side of Mount Everest they were going to scale? Of course not. That's ridiculous.

Yet that is precisely what millions of people do in their attitude toward their personal development. They fly by the seat of their pants, with no commitments, no goals, and no plans. Life is a toss up for them.

Why would anybody do that? There are two reasons. First, they just don't take life seriously enough. They are ambivalent about their goals. I don't see how anybody can be ambivalent in some circumstances. For instance, while at a football game I rooted for U.S.C., which wiped out its opponent, Michigan. The next morning I met a good friend who had also been at the game, and I said, "Wasn't that a great game?" "Yes," he grunted. Then I remembered something and I was embarrassed. "Ray," I said, "I'm sorry, I forgot you were rooting for Michigan." "No," he replied, "I was really ambivalent." "Ray, you should know," I explained, "that when you go to a football game you can't be ambivalent. I mean, you have to psych yourself up to either root for one side or the other, right?"

I may not be right. Perhaps you can be ambivalent in a football game, but don't ever be ambivalent about life. People who accomplish things have a singleness of purpose. They don't run with the hares and dash with the hounds. They take life seriously!

There's another reason why some people take the toss approach toward life: They take life too seriously. They take life so seriously that they are afraid of failure, defeat, being hurt, or rejection. They handle that potential fear by saying, "Well, I don't care. It isn't that bad anyway." Their I-don't-care attitude is really a phony defense mechanism because they care too much. Even though people take life too seriously, they must pretend they are not doing so. They reason that if they should lose, they can always say, "It didn't mean that much to me anyway." These people are dishonest. They take life so seriously that they build their strategy on their expected potential defeats.

Not long ago I talked to a young man in his early

twenties. He's a wonderful fellow and a good friend. Last year his marriage ended in divorce. Now he's facing the new year single—divorced. "I hope this is going to be the happiest year of your life," I said. Tears came to his eyes. I gave him the following advice: *"Build on your hopes. Don't build on your hurts."* You don't build your future on your disasters; you build your future on your dreams.

Everybody has his or her hurts and setbacks. Everybody experiences rejection. If you build on these hurts, you're going to take the flippant toss attitude and say, "I don't care about it." That's a mind-set focused on new failures. "Who cares?" That's the toss approach.

Do you see the contradiction here? Such people choose not to choose. And so the nonchoice becomes the choice. "Let's just flip a coin." No wonder they fail. You can be sure that's no path to the peak; yet that's the path many people choose.

II. BOSS

The second approach to the top I call the *boss* approach. These people take the attitude, "Don't tell me what to do. I know what I want to do," or "Don't tell me that I can't climb up the south side of the mountain. I read a book once that said there were people who did it. So don't bother me with new information. Don't bother me with the facts. I've made up my mind."

Four types of persons fall into this category and take the boss path. First, there's the person who has a little bit of experience. The person with a little experience tends to be a boss because, as has often been said, a little learning is a dangerous thing. He or she will say, "I read a book about mountain climbing. I know how to climb mountains."

The second kind of person who takes the boss approach is the one with too much experience. If a little learning is a dangerous thing, then a lot of experience is just as dangerous. You know this won't work or that won't work, for you tried it in the past and failed. That's your problem. You think you know it all and this results in locked-in thinking.

There are new inventions which must be taken into consideration. There are new kinds of steel pegs that can be driven into mountains that they didn't have when you were climbing. There are new kinds of ropes they didn't have when you were climbing. You just haven't kept up with the times.

You may say, "I know the organization will have nothing to do with this idea," or "I have dealt with the organization a hundred times in the past ten years." Wait a minute. How do you know? Maybe the board has changed. Maybe they have a new manager. Or perhaps that manager has changed his mind.

There is a third kind of person who takes the boss approach. He insists on having his own way all the time. There are times when leaders are inclined to be that way until they are struck with the ageless truth, *"It's more important to be right than to have your own way,"* or with another revelation: *"It's more important to be successful than to have your own way,"* or, to put it another way, "I'd rather not fail than have my will prevail." Great accomplishments happen to a person who doesn't insist on having his own way all the time.

Affirm the following now: I'd rather be stopped from making a wrong decision than have my own way.

EGO-INVOLVED OR SUCCESS-ORIENTED?

The fourth kind of person who takes the boss approach doesn't know how to change his or her mind. That's the kind of person who can't back out of a decision and doesn't want to lose face. He has told everyone what he was going to do, and he thinks he'll lose face if he switches course. I'd rather switch course and arrive at port safely than save face and sink at sea. If I ever were captain of a ship, I'd rather be embarrassed at port and admit I'd forgotten something than ignore the ego-damaging warning and be proven wrong at high sea, far from help.

In an earlier chapter I stated:

"People who never change their minds are either perfect or stubborn."

Nobody is perfect. And who wants to admit being stubborn? No one. So when you change your mind, what do you do? Lose face? Not at all. You earn respect. You demonstrate and expose yourself as an imperfect and nonstubborn person. If you follow that mental process, you won't lose face when you change your mind. You gain face because people see quality and character in your kind of honesty.

III. CROSS

The third approach is the only successful way to the peak, and that's the *cross* approach. What do I mean by the cross approach? I mean the challenge to sacrifice. There's no success without sacrifice. By the cross approach I mean self-denial. There's no success without self-denial. Yet, as I study successful persons whose lives reflect a movement from one peak to another, I see something deeper than sacrifice, self-denial, and struggle. The real synonym for the word "cross" is the word "humility."

What does humility mean? Is it the opposite of pride? Not necessarily. True humility is a form of pride. It is what I call sacrificial pride. And you're never going to climb to the top of the mountain of success unless you have enough humility to do two things: (1) admit to yourself that you need help, and (2) ask someone else to help you. No person can achieve success alone. It's impossible. Even an artist in an attic has to have somebody willing to buy his paintings.

The voice of humility says, "I need help." To the alcoholic the greatest peak experience would be to be dry.

But there can be no success until there is enough humility to say, "I'm an alcoholic. I need help." The proud person doesn't want to admit that he needs advice or counsel. And he is the loser!

While working toward my undergraduate degree at Hope College, I did very well except for first-year-mathematics. I almost failed because I didn't want to admit that I didn't know what the teacher was talking about. I was academically deprived when it came to mathematics. I had no background in geometry. The professor was teaching geometric principles and I didn't know what they were. I didn't want to put my hand up to ask a question because it looked like everybody else in the class understood him. I wasn't going to be the only stupid guy in the class. I figured I'd find out later. Later was almost too late. Until I was willing to admit I needed help, I was not going to grow. Humility is to ask for help.

Why is it so hard for us to ask for help? Is it because we don't want to admit we lack knowledge? Or are we afraid of being turned down, put down, or torn down? Why do people dare to set big goals? Are there people who are afraid of thinking big, talking big, or trying big? The humble people? Selfish pride leads to ruin. The person who never thinks big, talks big, or tries big isn't being humble. He is probably so proud that he is simply not going to risk failure by thinking big, talking big, and trying big. That's how selfish pride leads to failure!

If pride prevents you from succeeding, you are very selfishly going to prevent yourself from being the helpful person you could be. Then failure becomes doubly selfish!

By contrast, sacrificial pride is the strong self-confidence that believes it can succeed and dares to sacrifice its arrogance on the altar of some noble attempt, unashamedly calling out for all the help it can attract along the way.

So that's how sacrificial pride leads to success!

The person who reaches his mountaintop takes the cross approach and has enough humility to (1) risk failure, (2) ask for help, and (3) dare to be embarrassed in order to realize the human-need filling goal of unselfish success.

What is your dream? Your mountain? Your peak? Is

it hidden behind a cloud? It may be fighting alcoholism or going back to school. Perhaps it's graduating, getting a better grade, or patching up your marriage. Believe me, the cross approach is the only way.

chapter eight

Enthusiasm for the Peak

THE KEY TO SUCCESSFUL CLIMBING is tapping into the dynamic energy called enthusiasm. There are two energy forces: positive energy and negative energy.

The story is told of a man who was hired to dig graves in a cemetery. He had never done this before, so he dug graves that were either too wide, too long, or too deep. The old man finished just as the sun was going down. Weary from the long day, he sat down and leaned against the wall of one dark hole and fell asleep. Meanwhile, a man wandering through the cemetery fell into the grave. Frightened and panicky, he reached up as far as he could, trying to pull himself out. But each time he tried, he fell back into the dark, cold hole.

"Will I ever get out of here?" he cried out. And that awakened the gravedigger, who said from his dark corner. "Who's there?" And suddenly the other fellow got out!

That's what we call negative energy.

There are countless stories of people who have done seemingly impossible feats in times of fear or crisis.

Negative energy is that energy which grows out of negative thoughts and negative feelings.

Parents often try to energize and motivate their teenage children by unwittingly using negative energy-producing forces such as guilt, fear, intimidation, and threats. But negative energy doesn't last, for this type of energy leaves fatigue in its wake.

Negative energy is also stimulated by the use of intimidation or threats in vast organizations, institutions, and corporations. The latter often thrive on energy that is primarily stimulated by these negative means, in the hope that they might possibly motivate employees. (And leaders wonder why the basic output is so limited in relation to man-hours invested!) Negative energy is eventually self-defeating since it is stimulated by fear.

It's amazing how many people live their lives with an energy output that has its origin in a negative source. The end result is often high blood pressure, nervous breakdowns, ulcers, and heart trouble. Negative energy is destructive to the mind, the emotions, the nervous system, blood vessels, and to the heart.

In contrast to negative energy there is positive energy. Whether climbing your mountain literally means climbing moutains like the Himalayas or climbing mountains of obstacles, success depends on positive energy that enables you to stick with it.

Energy that is positive is energy fed by enthusiasm. Enthusiasm produces such positive energy that even when you're physically exhausted you can't wait to wake up the next morning to climb to a higher ledge. Positive energy moves you forward. Enthusiasm lifts you higher. Success becomes self-perpetuating.

Negative energy fatigues you, but positive energy replenishes you. Positive energy becomes a self-propagating force that knows no end. You achieve a new peak experience and from the new peak experience you are so exhilarated that you become confident that you can do even more than you thought. You see a new peak, so you begin to reach for it. When you reach that peak you receive a larger vision. The larger vision releases more enthusiasm. The new enthusiasm releases more energy. And you have a success cycle going that nothing can stop. Each new achievement only intensifies your energy capacity because it whips up more enthusiasm. That's the key.

Positive energy is released through enthusiasm that comes from the dynamic commitment to ideas that hold within themselves great possibilities and great potential to help people. So enthusiasm is a positive form of energy! It is the energy to (a) start projects, (b) sustain projects, (c) strengthen projects, and (d) succeed in projects.

Where does all this energy come from? From thoughts, and thoughts produce feelings, and feelings produce a physical reaction. If the thought is negative, the result is going to be a negative feeling. The physical reaction is going to be one of fatigue. If the thought is a possibility thought loaded with great potential, that thought will produce feelings that are positive and filled with enthusiasm! And that enthusiasm produces a physical reaction of vitality. You see it in the skin. You see it in the eyes. You feel it in the bloodstream. You feel it in the muscles. It is the source of a vital life! You can keep enthusiasm going as you keep possibility thoughts constantly flowing through your mind.

Here's how positive energy produces more enthusiasm. Your enthusiasm gets you started and you start climbing! As you start climbing, you have a peak experience, and when you have a peak experience you aim at a higher peak and you get enthusiastic about that! The Peak to Peek Principle! When you get to the higher peak, you dream greater dreams, set greater goals, and discover greater ideas. Enthusiasm is a positive, self-propagating, dynamic, self-expanding energy that flows from a positive thought or a positive idea.

Now, *there are four very important principles on* how to test the enthusiasm-generating potential in an idea. Four qualities are needed in any project or idea to keep the flow of enthusiasm going.

I. INTEGRITY

The first quality is *integrity*. There can be no enthusiasm in anything that you are promoting, projecting, planning, or striving toward unless it has total integrity. How many people do you know who don't have enough enthusiasm! A major reason for this is that many people are not totally honest in their private lives. If you harbor dark, black secrets, or if you're not totally honest, you cannot be enthusiastic, for enthusiasm is the practice of emotional freedom. Guilty persons dare not be emotionally liberated. They must become emotionally retrained or they just might "let the cat out of the bag" and "expose their dishonesty."

So the person who isn't honest definitely develops a subconscious emotional shell around his deeper emotions. People who, at their core, are dishonest, phony, flaky, or synthetic develop an emotional personality that restrains them from being bubbly and open. They cultivate an icy, chilly shell around their emotional selves. This shelters them from becoming the totally open persons who could expose their phoniness. That's why the hypocrite can never be a success. He lacks emotional power and energy that comes from enthusiasm! So only honest persons develop naturally into sincerely enthusiastic people. Integrity therefore must be at the core of your life. That's the first quality.

II. BE EXTRA-ORDINARY

The second enthusiasm-producing quality in a project, idea, or person is the capacity for being *extraordinary*. The commonplace is no turn-on. The word "enthusiasm" comes from the Greek words *en theos*, which, freely translated, mean "in God." God flows into human lives through constructive, creative ideas. God's ideas flowing through human minds are always aimed at revealing and realizing our undetected or underdeveloped potential. And enthusiasm is stimulated when the human mind is invaded by an idea that challenges it to grow. I believe that God structured the enthusiasm-generating system this way because God knows every living human being should be doing more than he's doing, thinking bigger than he's thinking, and planning more than he's planning. God knows that every living human being, whether he's four years old or ninety years old, still has to battle against the temptation to be lazy, to play it safe and avoid risks.

Growing is a part of life. There can be no stimulation unless there is the capacity for growth. This growth may be in quality, but growth potential must exist. Growth is essential, and that means the idea must be extra-ordinary. I'm sure that a mountain climber who has scaled a twenty-four-thousand-foot peak would no longer be excited by a foothill in California.

The capacity to be extra-ordinary—a little more or a little better than last time—is a quality that fosters and causes the flow of divine enthusiasm.

III. POSSESS EGO-FULFILLMENT POTENTIAL

A third essential enthusiasm-generating quality is *ego-fulfillment potential*. Before any idea, project, or peak challenge can generate enthusiasm, it must hold the promise of ego fulfillment. Ego fulfillment means that if I succeed in climbing the peak I will have a tremendous birth of self-worth.

This ego-fulfilling need is theological as well as psychological. You are a human being and not an ape. Human beings are made in the image of God. We are called the children of God in the Bible. We are royalty.

Because we have royal blood, we are not fulfilled until we have a feeling of sanctified pride. That's what drives this endless need for ego fulfillment.

I've heard many people put down others with the simplistic insult, "They're on an ego trip," as if ego fulfillment is naturally, automatically sinful.

The remark "He's on an ego trip" doesn't necessarily mean a person is conceited. The truth is that every human being needs ego fulfillment. Everybody needs an ego trip. To deny this is to fail to understand every person's drive to dignity, which is his or her instinctive divine inheritance as a member of the human race. If there is no self-esteem-boosting possibility, no ego fulfillment, then there will be no enthusiasm.

IV. SACRIFICIAL SERVICE

The final enthusiasm-generating quality that must be inherent in the "Peak Pursuing Project" is altruistic ego fulfillment. Ego-tripping is indeed dangerous, potentially demonic, and ultimately self-defeating unless it is conceived and executed with a purpose of sacrificially serving others.

I am on an ego trip. I derive great personal fulfillment from my ministry. But it only results to the degree that I give of myself as a pastor by helping people. I had a beautiful experience recently. I paid a hospital visit to a friend who was eighty-two years of age and had been a member of my church for eighteen years. It was a cold and rainy night and I selfishly wanted to stay at home by the cozy fire. But my friend was very sick, so I drove to the hospital. As I entered his room, I saw his lips trembling and his eyes filling with tears.

"Hello, Bob," he whispered softly. We prayed together and talked about heaven. Before I left the room, I took both of his feeble hands and said, "What can I do for you?" "Bob," he said, "just keep on being my friend. Just keep on loving me."

I found my ego fulfillment as I gave him my love and received love in return. I knew when I left that hospital that I had helped somebody who's coming to the end of the road. And there's no better feeling than that. It was the perfect feeling of self-esteem. I helped someone who needed help. In that moment I realized my peak: a child of God. And you can experience that wonderful feeling of redeemed pride which is real humility. Although it sounds like a contradiction, it is true. You will get that ego fulfillment safely when it results from sacrifice.

V. THE CROSS PURIFIES THE EGO TRIP

Let love flow through you—by denying your own pleasure, giving up some of the pleasure—seeking time, and committing yourself to being involved in somebody else's life—and the sacrificial element will sanctify the ego trip. It is the cross that turns the ego trip into a safe, satisfactory, and sanctified experience instead of a demonic experience.

It is the dying of the self through involving yourself that purges the ego trip of its potential demonic temptations and turns it into a miracle of God's goodness.

Possibility thinking will keep your enthusiasm going if the possibility-thinking ideas possess integrity, a capacity for being extra-ordinary, ego fulfillment, and service to others.

Show me a person who's really dynamic and alive with exciting energy and I'll show you a person who's turned on by God's ideas. God's ideas are loaded with far more possibilities than we ever suspected. When we are in God and God is within us, then fantastic ideas come to us. His ideas are loaded with possibilities. These possibilities stimulate us with great positive expectations. No wonder our enthusiasm never dries up. And we have, in fact, tapped into an energy power that can and will see us all the way to the top of the mountain.

So the Peak to Peek Principle finds its power in the energy that flows from God through dynamic ideas. These ideas will:

(1) display integrity
(2) be extra-ordinary
(3) hold forth the promise of ego fulfillment
(4) demand enough self-sacrifice to guarantee enough humility so that God can trust you with success.

chapter nine

Stamina Unlimited

QUESTION: HAVE YOU EVER FACED a challenging idea only to turn away from it? Do you know why you didn't risk the opportunity?

Question: What is it that keeps us from seeking the peak experiences of life? Why is it that so many people run away from problems instead of pursuing the great opportunities in life that would give them a mountaintop experience and leave them with greater self-confidence and assurance? There are several answers to these questions.

Answer 1: "Well, I suppose people avoid the mountaintop experience because they are afraid of the struggle." Yes, that's part of the answer, but there is more.

Answer 2: "Well, people prefer the ease and comfort of living in the valley." That answer is partly true, but there is still more.

Answer 3: "They avoid the mountaintops because they just don't want to risk failure." That is also true. But there is more!

At the deepest level, people turn away from opportunities, possibilities, and success because *they just don't think they have the stamina to see themselves through to the very top*. They are not confident that they have the resources for the climb. They say, "What if I make a commitment and then find myself halfway up the mountain, exhausted and depleted of my resources?"

There are three sources of water in California: reservoirs, wells, and springs. In northern California there are times when the reservoirs are dry and empty. But these reservoirs are really not sources of water, just gathering places.

Is it possible that you may be backing away from great opportunities because you don't think you have what it takes to make it to the top, because you're not sure you have the inner resources (emotional, physical, and spiritual) and you don't want to get halfway up the mountain and run out of gas? Is it because you just don't think you've got what it takes? Then you may be backing away from the challenge because your major source of nourishment is a *reservoir*. You're tapping your own human experiences and energy, and that has severe limitations! The truth is that you and I don't have what it takes to scale the peaks if we just depend on our own strength! If you depend on a reservoir to supply your resources, you'll run out of steam.

There's a second source of water in California, and that's the well. Wells are better than reservoirs because they tap the underground water table. But sometimes we have a problem in California because the water table has dropped so low that water no longer seeps into some of the wells and they run dry.

There are people who try to draw their energy and stamina for success not from the reservoir of their experience and knowledge but from the well of their inheritance—the family and tradition. The latter can be an enormous source of emotional nurture, but watch out: Wells can run dry too!

A third source of water is the mountain spring fed by the snow-capped glaciers that never thaw. *The spring flows from the snow-capped mountaintop!*

When you tap the spring of God's energetic flow, you have emotional power. That means power to feed enthusiasm, power to think positive thoughts, power to push negative thoughts out, power to maintain peace under enormous pressure.

You can have stamina unlimited! When you've tapped the spring, you don't trust your own strength! That's a reservoir! You can't just depend upon business associates, friends, or family. That's a well. You have the mountaintop spring! You are connected with Almighty God!

Stop running away from opportunities and possibilities! Run toward fulfillment, actualization, and success!

You may have heard of Abraham Maslow, one of the great psychologists of this century. I find myself in tune with many things he has said. He projected the idea of the "Jonah complex." Certainly everybody would like to be better than they are, Maslow noted. We all have within us an impulse to improve ourselves, an impulse toward actualizing our possibilities. Then what holds us back? What blocks us? He called this restraining force the Jonah complex. He described how Jonah ran away from God, turning his back on the great possibilities that God had lined up for him.

What does the Jonah complex mean? Simply this: It is a fear of our own greatness; the evasion of one's high destiny; the deliberate choice of running away from our best talents. We fear the best more than we fear the worst. We can stand the presence of somebody far below us morally and not be afraid, but when we stand in the presence of somebody morally upright, we are uncomfortable. *We fear our highest potential!* Why do we evade our own possibilities? Because there is a universal fear of an encounter with God. Maslow called it "counter valuing"—the fear of a direct confrontation with God. We fear running into God just as we fear running into our own opportunities and possibilities. So we back away from all of it.

Not long ago I had four tremendous possibilities thrown at me, possibilities that unquestionably are great opportunities. As I was jogging one morning, I began my usual conversation with God. "Lord, I have enough to do. I've got this whole church. I've got a book being published this year and the weekly 'Hour of Power' broadcast. Lord, I have enough hay on the fork. Projects require money. All of them require energy, too. I don't know if I've got the stamina." "You can choose to fail these projects," God said to me. "No one will ever know. But many people will not be benefited as they would if you take these new challenges!"

Well, that night I went to bed early, hoping to get a good night's rest, but I woke up in the middle of the night. Negative thoughts came to my mind as they seldom have before. I remembered my dreams of twenty-five years ago, when I came to California with nothing except a call from God to begin a church. A dream! The price of leadership was difficult then—and still is. Costly commitments, pressure, the risk of failure, criticism, fear of being misunderstood and having your motives held in question.

Often, the only thing you can do is agree with Plato's statement, "I will live in such a way that I will prove by my life that my critics are liars."

I was unable to sleep, and negative thoughts began to attack me until it was almost as if a panic waited at my bedside to overwhelm me. At that point I prayed this deep prayer: "O God, four great opportunities have been thrown before me. I didn't ask for them. Lord, if the ideas came from you, and you want me to fulfill them, please give me the strength to handle them and the peace of mind to know that it is right. And Lord, unless you give me the strength, you have to let me pull out, back up, and abort all four opportunities. Nobody will ever know. It's up to you, Lord. I don't want to say, 'Schuller, you didn't have the faith.'"

Then I was stretched out flat on my back. I relaxed completely until I was unconscious of my body, which seemed to float. It was an absolute, transcendent feeling of peace that I can only describe as an experience of eternal life, a pure soul at total peace. I sensed I was suspended in the presence, peace, and power of my God. A power beyond myself, power of mind, power of heart, power of body. I experienced a fantastic power that I believe came from God. I have never in my life felt so strong. At that moment I knew the decision I had to make. I made the commitment—and I succeeded!

You can have this power, too, if you will draw close to God.

Stamina unlimited. What a claim! There is a cosmic

intelligence, energy, and vitality called God. He promises a supply of energy and power that gives us stamina unlimited. I have only one central lesson I want you to derive from this, the shortest but perhaps the most important lesson in the book. Here it is: "God's got the power if you've got the faith." No person is too small for God's love, and no peak is too high for you to climb.

chapter ten

Why People Choose to Fail

I SUSPECT THAT AT THE END OF MY LIFE somebody may say, "Schuller was a big failure . . . in golf!" And that's true. I used to play golf, but I was so terrible I gave it up. I quit. Someone might also say that I was a failure in tennis. And that would be true too. But *I have chosen to be a failure* in these sports. I have chosen to divert my time and energies to other areas. You succeed or fail based on the decisions you make.

If you fail, it is because you choose to fail.

Why do people choose to fail? What keeps a person from making the choice to climb the mountain that could assure him a peak experience?

Theologians agree that we are put into this world to glorify God and enjoy Him forever. That is sound theology. And to this sound theological concept we have wedded the following most harmonious psychological truth: Until you develop your God-given potential and possibilities in an achievement experience, your life will fail to glorify God as it could and should. So the person who feels that he's a failure has an intuitive suspicion that he's really not glorifying God the way he ought to.

Tom Lasorda, manager of the Los Angeles Dodgers, has a story that he likes to tell. He was a manager in the minor leagues in 1971, when his team lost seven straight games. About that time the sports writers across the country had voted to select the greatest major league team in the history of baseball. By a vast majority vote the honor went to the 1927 Yankees.

Defeated and exhausted, Tom's losing team headed for the locker room. A few minutes later he walked in and found all the players sitting around, dejected, with their heads down. "Hey, get your heads up!" Tom yelled. "I don't ever want to see you fellows with your heads down again. Just because you lost seven games doesn't mean you're not a great team. You're going to start winning! As you know, according to a recent poll, the greatest team to ever play in the major leagues was the Yankees in 1927. And they lost nine straight games!" Suddenly heads went up and expressions changed. It was the turning point. The team started winning, and by the end of the season they were the champions!

A few days later Mrs. Lasorda asked, "Tommy, are you sure the Yankees lost nine games in a row?" "How would I know?" Tom answered. "I was only a year old. But it made the point." The team had to believe in themselves. They had to believe they could do it!

What you believe will determine the decisions you make. And the decisions you make will determine whether you have a peak experience or whether you live down in the valley. Whether you succeed or fail depends on the choices you make. You might say, "Yes, but there are people who have problems and unforeseen emergencies that come up." Even then you choose how to react! And your reaction will be your conscious or subconscious decision to succeed or fail.

Let me give you some words that will help you understand why people fail.

First, some people fail because they are *wired* wrong. They have a bad connection. They are hooked up to a negative input. They connect themselves to negative thinkers. They have no connection with God. Yes, even pious, evangelical, orthodox religious people are not immune to negative thinking. You may know the Bible and not have a vital relationship with the living, loving God who wants to lift you and lead you to mountaintops. He wants to give you an abundant life now. He wants to fill you with a constant flow of positive thoughts.

If I am not dreaming great dreams, I ask myself, "Am I wired right? Is my connection plugged into a positive source?" Some people are just wired wrong.

Others choose to fail because they have *expired*. They have given up. They let their dream die and they tell themselves, "I can't make it." Under the dust storm of discouragement their dreams were allowed to suffocate into depression, discouragement, and disappointment.

Friends often say to me, "Schuller, I hope you live to see all your dreams come true!" "I hope I don't, or I will have died before I die," I answer, "because you die when you stop dreaming."

Dreams keep you alive. If you don't have dreams that are beyond your grasp, you've already started to die. *That's why the point of arriving is far more dangerous than the process of becoming.*

You expire when you stop dreaming. If you are in that category today, let me remind you of something. People can frustrate you. They can be obstacles. But you alone, of all human beings, have the power to kill your dream. Others can suffocate it, blanket it, strangle it, block it, or fence it in, but you are the only one who finally says, "I give up." Others may lead you to the edge of defeat, but you are the one who decides to accept failure.

Since some people choose to fail because they are wired wrong and others because they are expired, what is the third reason? It is because they are *retired*.

They have had it! They don't need to earn any more money. They don't care to accomplish anything else. They don't want to reach any further. They have had their successes. A minister once said to me at one of our institutes in church development, "I'm really not interested in success."

I was puzzled. "Are you interested in failure?" I replied.

"No, I don't care about success or failure," he said. "Schuller, you seem to be very interested in success.

Apparently you're trying to prove something to yourself or somebody. I don't need to prove anything to anybody."

"It's not a question of proving anything to anybody," I enthused, "but to prove to God that you want your life to count for something great, and to people that you care about them." That's the point.

What's the purpose of life? To glorify God and enjoy Him! God wants you to succeed! Success is building self-esteem in yourself and others through sincere service. Success is not selfish. Failure is the selfish objective in life, for when you choose to fail you fail because you choose not to pay the price to succeed. I know people who retire for good. These people don't feel a need to accomplish anything more in life. Why take the risk? Why be an adventuresome person anymore if the work is too demanding? Basically, these people are lazy. The price is too high. If you don't want to put out any more than you have to, you will choose to fail. So you won't have any more peak experiences.

I can't see retiring. Keep active! Keep setting new goals! Live within your new limits, but continue to create new peak experiences of personal achievement.

There is a fourth reason why people choose to fail. It is because they are *fired*. They got laid off. They tried but got kicked out. They've been hurt. People don't appreciate them. Maybe they didn't get support when they needed it, so now they are angry.

In the movie *The Loneliness of the Long Distance Runner* a young student signed up for a track team and developed a personality conflict with the coach. This relationship became filled with hostility. On the day of the championship race, the runner started off fast, leading the whole pack. He was well in the lead and only about twelve feet from the finish line when he stopped. The others ran past him and finished the race. The losing runner walked over to his stunned coach and said, "You didn't deserve to get my trophy." The student deliberately chose to lose the race because he was fired with anger and hatred at his coach.

Only God knows how many people are not conquering new peaks *because of fierce anger* directed at a husband, a wife, a father, a mother, a sister, a boss, a professor, a coach, or the company!

It's hard to tell how many people choose to fail because they are angry at God, at the world, or at life. How many people are still choosing to fail because they are trying to get even with somebody? A student may retaliate against a professor and try for a low grade because he wants to prove that the teacher is a terrible instructor. A teammate may do a terrible job on the field because he's mad at another player. He wants to punish the rest of the team because he didn't get his own way.

So people choose to fail because they are wired, expired, retired, or fired. Still others fail because they are *mired*— mired in a muddy road of negative thoughts! They are stuck in a rut. They don't seek mountaintops. They don't set new goals or make big decisions. They've got a secure job and they don't ever want to change. A rut is nothing more than a grave with the ends knocked out.

Some people are *mired in their guilt*. These people choose to fail because they don't believe they deserve to succeed.

This very distorted belief represents an attempt to atone for guilt. It is rooted in the idea that failure will demonstrate humility. They believe that if they are humble in their losses God will love them because of their humility.

You glorify God in humility, but the greatest humility of all is to be humble enough to commit yourself to a failure-potential project that will do somebody good. That's the way to be humble and glorify God.

When you've had an authentic experience of God's forgiving grace and salvation, you are liberated from guilt. You are adopted into God's family as his child.

Others are mired in *self-condemning thoughts*. They don't know how to win except by losing. Some family members may try to inspire them to be A students or to go on to college or to hit a new peak. "I don't have it," is the response, and so, of course, nothing is achieved.

And by not achieving what they said they could not achieve they feel they have at least succeeded as a negative prophet. So the only way that some people know how to win is to plan to lose. Then they can say, "See, I told you I couldn't do it." They don't want to lose, so they never enter the contest. If you never run the race, then you'll never lose, right? Wrong! You will lose what you could have won.

Some people fail because of the way they are *attired*. They are too dignified to try. They are "culturally attired" in a false dignity that will not permit them to adopt a strategy that would be sure to succeed.

I know of a young preacher who was so intellectually snobbish that he refused to compromise his multisyllabic words and simplify his language and his style so that he could successfully communicate to the ordinary person. As a result, he failed miserably as a preacher. He then took a job as a professor in a classroom, where he spent a great deal of time criticizing "corny preachers in the pulpit."

There can be no success without reasonable compromise—of intelligence or cultural taste. Consider the young man who insisted on wearing tattered jeans with an old shirt and long, uncombed hair to his job. Because he worked in a place that had to effectively communicate with persons of a different cultural level, he was told to "dress up or get out." He got out. The company even offered to buy him clothes. He thought he was too dignified to switch clothes. In reality, he was too stubborn.

Then there are those who choose to fail because they have simply *hired* themselves out. They have sold out their glorious dreams. You've heard people say, "There must be an easier way to make a living."

There's a story in the Bible about a Shepherd who hired a man to care for his sheep. But this temporary helper failed at the job. He wasn't about to risk his life to save a sheep. "Let the wolves attack," he said. Why? The hired man didn't own the sheep. He was just filling in for the shepherd. The herdsman was the original owner. He would lay down his life for the animals because they were his sheep.

We all know people who choose to fail because they have this negative attitude toward life. They check into a motel and don't bother to take good care of the room; after all it isn't their property. They take that same attitude toward their God-given dreams. They take that same attitude toward opportunity. They take that same attitude toward possibilities. They've sold out on their greater values. They don't want to pay the price to reach the peak. It's that simple. They choose to fail.

I had the honor of participating in the commencement activities at Pepperdine University, in Malibu, California. There were probably a hundred or more students who received their B.A. degree that night. The audience was made up of a collection of beautiful people. About three-fourths of them were non-Caucasian. Most of these were American blacks. The average age of these college graduates was close to forty. It was a truly beautiful experience watching the graduates walk across the stage to receive their degrees from the president of the university.

Among the graduates was a sixty-seven-year-old mother of ten children and grandmother of twenty-seven grandchildren. When that determined woman stepped onto the stage to receive her diploma, an older man and several children jumped up from their seats and began to applaud. "You did it, Mama!" they screamed. "You did it, Grandma!" When the newly graduated sixty-seven-year-old grandmother met me afterward, she gave me a big hug and said, "If it hadn't been for my faith and your possibility thinking, I wouldn't have made it." She was so proud of herself. And her family was proud of her too. That was a peak experience, for it left her with great self-esteem.

What a beautiful illustration of God's reward to the person who's made the decision not to fail anymore, but to choose to be a success for the glory of God! That's what you call self-esteem! God wants you to succeed!

Were you on a winning path but decided to switch to

ditch? Choose to stop failing and choose to start succeeding!

Are you wired wrong? Get wired right. Be connected to God. He'll give you a bigger dream! He'll give you a new goal! He'll give you something to strive for! Of course it will be risky. There will be a price tag! If there's no risk or price tag, it won't mean anything. So move out! Choose to succeed!

chapter eleven

Turn Your Weak Times into Peak Times

EVERY PROBLEM IS A POTENTIAL OPPORTUNITY. You can draw great dividends from your deepest difficulties if you understand the possibility-thinking perspective on life. Possibility thinkers see every problem as a potential project. When you begin to see the problem as a project, the project produces enthusiasm, and enthusiasm produces success! It's all a matter of making the decision to choose to respond positively to whatever happens to you. This means any weak time can be turned into a peak time if you keep the possibility-thinking perspective. It's that incredibly simple!

There are no projects unless there are problems, no conversion without crisis, no resurrection without death. That's why possibility thinkers are not Pollyanna people. They have a profound grasp of the universal principle for dynamic living!

A beautiful illustration of turning your weak times into peak times is found in the Psalms:

> Happy are those who are strong in the Lord,
> who want above all else to follow your steps.
>
> When they walk through the Valley of Weeping
> it will become a place of springs

where pools of blessing and refreshment collect
after the rains.
(Psalms 84:5,6)

In my book *Reach Out for a New Life* I told a story
about a good friend, Asa Skinner. I received a call one
day—I was at our home in a Chicago suburb—telling
me that Asa had fainted at work and friends had taken
him to the hospital. After tests were run, the diagnosis
was conclusive: a blood clot in the brain. Doctors oper-
ated successfully but Asa was told he'd be confined to a
wheelchair for the rest of his life. At sixty-six years of
age he would no longer be able to work. At first he was
terribly depressed. Suicidal thoughts went through his
mind. But soon his faith was strengthened. He refused
to surrender to negative thoughts. He began thinking
positively.

I shall never forget the day that I called on him. He
was home now and I thought he would be resting
inside. I rang the doorbell and his wife, Nina, answered
the door. "Is Asa around?" I asked. "He's in the backyard; go on around," she said. I opened the gate and
went into the backyard unannounced. He was slumped
over in a wheelchair, motionless. I approached him
quietly from the side and couldn't believe what I saw.
Asa was looking at the ground through binoculars. And
on his lap was a pad filled with notes. "Hello, Asa," I
shouted. "SHHHHH!" he whispered, adding, "don't dis-
turb them." Puzzled, I leaned over and touched the
blades of grass where he'd been looking. Camouflaged
in the soil were hundreds of little red ants. Asa let the
glasses rest against his chest and looked up. "Bob," he
exclaimed, "they have really made headway today!"
Then he began to tell me about all of the living creatures in his backyard. There was a spider building a
web, ants gathering food, and birds feeding their young.
His confined world was teeming with life and excitement and adventure.

"Bob," he enthused, "I see love and peace, life and
death, and resurrection! New flowers are struggling so

they can grow and bloom! I don't think I have ever been more excited in my life than I am here, watching and discovering this world."

His weak time became a peak time. You can guess the rest. He recovered and went back to work and moved up to become chairman of the board of his company. When you go through the valley of trouble, it can turn out to be a spring of new life. Your weak times can become peak times.

Trouble never leaves you where it found you. It either changes you into a *better* person or a *bitter* person. You have the freedom to choose what your problem will do to you. The weak time can become your peak time.

One cantankerous old man lived as if he was mad at the whole world. Then one day he had a stroke, which left him paralyzed. Years later, when an old friend paid him a visit, the former didn't seem to be the same person. The grouchy old man had become mellow. His roughness had become smooth and gentle. His eyes, which had been hard as steel, had become warm and soft. The worn, wrinkled face, once tight and stiff, was glowing with warmth. Noticing the transformation in the old man's personality, the friend said, "Sickness and trouble have a way of coloring the personality, don't they?" The elderly man looked up at him and replied in a quiet and gentle voice, "Yes, sickness has a way of coloring the personality, and I decided that I would pick the colors and make them beautiful!"

Then there was the lady who telephoned and asked to see me. She had been an unbeliever most of her life until the year before. Her reason for calling was that she had terminal cancer and wanted to see me. She lived in a tiny apartment just a few miles from my office. She couldn't have weighed more than eighty pounds. She was skin and bones. I sat next to her bedside and looked into her eyes. What beauty! Her eyes twinkled! They were so youthful looking, too!

"Thank you for coming, Dr. Schuller," she said. "You brought faith into my life. I'm not afraid now. I know where I am going. Your possibility thinking has changed my attitude toward my sickness. I was bitter and angry at the world for so long. I was afflicted with self-pity and all these negative emotions until I turned them over to the Lord. That's when I thought about new possibilities for me. What could I possibly do for others in my condition? And I decided that I would try to minister to all the people who came to call on me. So, before anyone comes to visit I say a little prayer:

> Dear God,
> Help me to do something for them.
> Help me to cheer them up!

And do you know what? These have been the most exciting weeks of my life. When people come, I share the love of God with them and they leave knowing God really cares for them. Isn't that wonderful?"

God never lets anything happen to you unless it is loaded with opportunities.

Through faith, the weak times can become peak times.

chapter twelve

Fountains on the Mountains

ALLOW ME TO BEGIN THIS CHAPTER with three very important questions and answers.

(1) *What is failure?* It is not measured in dollars or material objects. Failure is reaching a point where you suddenly realize that you are not worth anything. Lack of self-esteem is the ultimate failure.

(2) *Why do most persons lack self-esteem?* They lack this quality because they fail to head for the mountains. They avoid challenging experiences which could give them mountaintop experiences to affirm to them that they can travel, struggle, and view life positively and courageously.

(3) *Why do people avoid the mountains?* Why do they avoid pursuing peak experiences? The answer is that they want to take it easy. They want to play it safe. People want possibilities without obstacles. They want to have a mountaintop experience down in the valley. You can't have one without the other. You can't have a peak experience if you're not willing to climb the mountain.

There are fountains on the mountains that you don't find in the valleys. There are fountains of bubbling self-esteem on top of the mountains that challenge us and call forth the best within us. There is no way you can achieve self-esteem short of struggle. There is no pride without commitment. There are no opportunities without obstacles.

If you want to have a peak experience, you have to look for the mountains. You have to take a possibility-thinking attitude toward mountains. Problems, difficulties, and pain are all mountains. Negative thinkers see mountains as dry, barren, energy-draining experiences. The possibility thinker sees them as hills with hidden springs that supply refreshing fountains of happy living. Persons with healthy self-esteem have made it their lifestyle to look for and welcome the mountains.

Mountains hold fountains of fruitful life-esteem-producing power.

Problems, like motors, generate power. The motor in a car generates energy either negatively or positively, depending on the driver. If it's in the hands of a negative driver, a careless accident may take his life. But that same motor can produce power to drive a doctor to make a life-saving call.

Problems produce energy. Negative energy is anxiety, worry, fear, jealousy, and self-pity, which all lead to fatigue. The motor sputters until you are emotionally out of gas. If you develop a positive mental attitude, that same problem produces an equal amount of energy, but instead of being channeled into worry, anxiety, and fear, it now produces courage, hope, and inspiration. Before you know it, the problem has become a peak. In this way problems produce power.

The mountain is an experience of potential power. The mountain is motivation. Give me mountains, for there are fountains on the mountains!

Let me describe some of the powers that flow from these energetic fountains.

I. BURNING POWER

First, mountains produce what I call *burning power*. I was talking to a very wealthy friend. I asked him how he became so wealthy.

"I was born in such poverty that I had a burning desire for wealth," he answered. "I abhorred poverty! The burning desire never left me," he continued. "That's why I am a rich man today!" The problem of poverty became a mountain that produced a fountain of inspiration to become wealthy.

"Along the way I found God," he added. "And He didn't dry up my consuming desire for wealth. He gave me the desire to be richer and richer, because He told me what good things I could do for Him if I made my millions." "What does being superwealthy make you feel like?" I asked. "It makes me feel powerful," he answered. "I have the power to help people like you!"

As a young child, my friend ran into a mountain called poverty. But because of that mountain his attitude changed. He took a positive attitude. He had a *burning* desire.

The president of Yale University advised another esteemed college president to always be kind to the A and B students because "someday they'll come back to the campus as professors," adding, "and treat C and D students with great affection because they are the ones who will come back someday to donate two million dollars to build the science building." It's really true! The average students want to prove to the world that they are as good as anybody else even though they didn't get A's and B's. Problems produce burning power.

II. CHURNING POWER

The second power is what I call *churning power*. While in Florida I met some people who were buying a home. "Why did you decide to move?" I asked. "It's a cold winter we're having up north," the wife answered. "I've been trying to get my husband to move to Florida for years, but he wouldn't budge until now."

Problems produce great churning power, which loosens the roots and unsettles you until finally you have to make a move. Most people don't move until they are pushed by a big problem. That's churning power!

III. TURNING POWER

Fountains on the mountains produce burning power, churning power, and then *turning power!* I recall a story about a small town in Alabama that built a monument to the boll weevil. It's incredible to hear about the ideas that some people come up with and how these ideas materialized.

Enterprise, Alabama, had been totally dependent on the cotton industry. One day disaster struck as the boll weevil wiped out the small town's entire crop. That catastrophe produced a conflict. The churning power produced turning power. It forced the town to think of other enterprises. It forced them to be creative, to see new possibilities. They diversified their industries and became so successful that the name Enterprise was more fitting than ever. Because they have a variety of industries, they no longer have to worry about crop failures. The community has prospered! Everybody realized the best friend they had was the boll weevil, so they built a monument to honor the insect. Marvelous! But that's turning power!

IV. LEARNING POWER

The fourth power produced by a problem is what I call *learning power*. People learn from their failures. They learn from problems. They learn from conflict.

A problem can be an opportunity for someone to start a business. There isn't a business in the world that could exist if there weren't problems. Companies should be thankful for problems because conflict guides and directs them to the source of the problem.

Speaking to a group of executive officers in an eastern state, I said, "If you are having a problem, you are making a mistake in one of these areas: manufacturing, marketing, merchandising, or management. *Your complaint department should become your quality control department*." With that positive attitude toward problems, they become fountains on the mountains.

Educators would be out of business if we were all

born *intuitively* brilliant. Doctors would be out of business if we were in perfect health. Church people would be out of business if everyone was possibility-thinking oriented. And policemen would be out of business if everyone was perfect.

Negative thinkers don't learn from problems because they run away from them. If you take a positive attitude toward problems, you can face them. Positive-thinking people expect problems. They see them as opportunities instead of obstacles. They are like an ant who was struggling with a heavy burden. This tiny creature was attempting to carry a big piece of straw. While maneuvering the heavy load, he came to a crack in the sidewalk. After several unsuccessful attempts to cross the crack, he swung the piece of straw around until it went right across the obstacle. And then he walked over the makeshift bridge to the other side.

He had turned his burden into a bridge!

V. EARNING POWER

To possibility thinkers mountains create burning power, churning power, turning power, learning power, and *earning power*.

There's a reason why possibility thinkers succeed in life. They know that necessity is the mother of invention. They see every problem as an opportunity.

Every burden can become a bridge. You will never grow unless you struggle. There is no gain without pain. There is no crown without a cross. It is so incredibly simple.

Why do people fail? They do so because they run away from the mountain. They don't want problems. They choose comfort.

You may know the story of Sadhu Sundar Singh, a well-known convert who became a missionary in India. In his writings he tells about becoming a Christian, rather than a Hindu or a Buddhist, because Christianity teaches you to go out into the world to seek the lost. He believed in looking for people with problems so he could love them and help them and save them. Many

Hindus live in monasteries and retreat from the world. They lose themselves in meditation instead of having day-to-day contact with people.

One day, Sadhu Sundar Singh and a Buddhist monk were traveling up a steep mountain on their way to a monastery. A blizzard threatened their lives as the chilly, icy winds blew through their thin clothes. "We must hurry because darkness is falling," the monk said. "The weather is bad and if it gets any worse we will soon freeze to death."

And so they moved as fast as they could through the blinding storm.

Suddenly they heard a cry for help. About twenty feet in front of them was the dim form of someone lying in the snow. "We must help," Sadhu exclaimed. "We cannot help," said the monk. "Fate has decreed that he must die. We have no time to spare or we will die!" So the monk went on while his companion, the Christian convert, insisted on helping his fallen brother.

If he must die, he would die saving someone. The figure in the snow was a man with a broken leg, so the Christian made a sling out of his blanket and dragged the dying man like a team of dogs pulling a sled. The passage was arduous and weary. He kept slipping and struggling up the mountain, fighting to stay alive. Suddenly he saw the blinking lights of the monastery. Now he was sure he could make it. Suddenly he stumbled and fell over something hidden beneath the snow. He brushed off the white powder and saw the frozen body of the Buddhist monk. Sadhu's life had been spared because he helped someone in need. He looked at a burden and saw it as an opportunity to show his love. Because he forgot himself, he survived.

Years later he was asked, "What is life's most difficult task?" Without hesitating he replied, "Life's most difficult task is to have no burden to carry."

Burdens become bridges.

When God gives you a mountain, it is one of the greatest gifts He could give you! For there's a glorious fountain in every mountain!

God promises you enough challenges and mountains

so that at the mature age of eighty-five, you will still have peaks to conquer. You will never run out of opportunities to conquer the mountains that continue to nourish your self-esteem.

chapter thirteen

Nest on the Crest

FINALLY, WHEN YOU STAND IN THE SUNLIGHT at the mountaintop of a successful experience, enjoy the moment! Taste the sweet wine of success. Here, now, at the top of the mountain, you will begin to believe that you can do anything. You'll envision bigger dreams. Believe in those new dreams!

Successful people have consciously or unconsciously tapped into the Peak to Peek Principle of prosperous living. A mountain-*peak* experience leaves you with a self-affirming awareness that you are more than you ever thought you were. You believe now that you can do more than you ever thought you could!

Why do some people find that one success leads to new and greater success, while others experience failure, which produces low achievement, giving rise to another defeat, until they are seemingly caught in a ghetto of personal failures and setbacks? What makes the difference? Successful persons, unlike the low achievers, have learned to live by the Peak to Peek Principle!

Failure-prone persons tend to make decisions in the valleys of life, while consistently successful persons have developed the habit of making decisions on the mountaintop. Learn their secret: *Nest on the crest!* Hatch out your plans in times of strength! Make major decisions in your healthy times, not in your times of sickness. Don't be like the entrapped person, who usually makes major

77

decisions in times of defeat. He doesn't nest on the crest, he nests in the swamp of despair. He doesn't move from strength but from weakness, which explains why he moves from one failure to another.

I'll never forget a counseling session I had several years ago with a defeated, brokenhearted man. His wife had just deserted him, and he was crushed. He was in the valley, not on a peak. "I'll tell you what I'm going to do, Dr. Schuller, and I've made up my mind," he exclaimed bitterly. "What's that?" I said. He listed his intentions for me: "One, I'm selling my business. Two, I'm moving out of California. Three, I'll never trust another woman. Four, I'll never make any more promises."

"You're going to sell your business?" I asked. "What are you going to do?" "I don't know," he replied. "That remains to be seen. It depends on where I go." "And you've decided to move out of California," I said. "Where are you going?" "I don't know," the man answered, "but I'm pulling out of here. When I reach my destination, I'll decide what I'm going to do." "And you're never going to make any promises or trust another woman? That means you'll never have any committed relationships. Is that what you're saying?" I asked. "You better believe it," he doggedly affirmed.

I said to my friend, "You are making one big mistake." Puzzled, he looked at me and asked, "What's that?" I told him, "You are making permanent, irreversible, negative decisions when you are at your emotional worst, not when you are at your emotional best. Right now, you are not in the best frame of mind. You are probably weaker than you have ever been. Here is one lesson you must learn: Never make negative decisions in dark times. Ride the storm out! Don't trust your judgment when you are down. See this storm through, but don't make any rash, irreversible, negative decisions when you are distressed."

"What do you mean?" he asked.

"It's quite simple," I explained. "You say your business has been doing well. Suppose, two years from now, things cool off and you wish you had your business back again. Can you pick it up just like that?" "I guess not," he said. "Suppose, in a year or two, you meet some beautiful woman and the two of you have the capacity to love and to trust each other. If you make a decision today that you're never going to give another person a chance to love and be loved by you, you'll deprive yourself of great joy."

One of the greatest tragedies of life is to make future plans in times of personal despair. This is nesting in the valley instead of on the mountaintop. This is hatching ideas out in reactionary moments of personal defeat or setback.

Failure-prone people are trapped in an emotionally deprived ghetto of underachievement, failure, and poverty. They are making decisions out of weakness, rather than out of strength. Don't nest in the valley; nest on the crest!

What do you do when you are in the slough, or in the valley, or in the bottom of the canyon? Just sit tight, keep hoping, and pray deeply. Believe that you'll get out of the valley! When you're strong and thinking at your best, that's the time for action! When you are down in the slough, do not believe in the shadows, or you will become entrapped as a child of darkness.

If you're in the valley today, don't make any negative decisions. And if you are on the edge of a *peak* experience, get ready, think big, strive to succeed. For success is the most unselfish objective you can have.

Never get caught running out of water if you're dashing across the desert.

Never get caught running out of gas if you're driving through the mountains.

Never get caught running out of air if you're skin diving.

Never get caught running out of food if you're an astronaut on a space voyage.

And never get caught running out of dreams if you want to travel meaningfully through life.

How do you nest on the crest?

What do you do on the top of the mountain? Three things:

I. LOOK OUT!

First, *look out* when you reach the top of a mountain, because you are surrounded by dangers! There are storms that swirl only at the tops of mountain peaks. Loose rocks could cause you to slip and fall down the mountain!

One of the great storms in life is learning to handle success.

It is difficult to handle recognition and acclaim. So the moment of success may become the beginning of the end. You may lose your humility or your drive or your compassion or your humanity or your team spirit when you reach the peak! Success can spoil you!

There are other dangers on the peak—unique dangers. Because you are at the top, you become known. And the high achievers are thrown inevitably into the role of expected leader. Those who still haven't made it to the top expect leadership from you. That's the price of success! You may fall victim to the jealousy of others in your family and community. Critics are bound to begin an assault. Success may force you to take sides where before you were able to remain anonymously uncommitted in the private safety of the masses.

But even though the peak is a time of danger, it is more than ever a time of opportunity! You have the opportunity to rise above the anxieties and pressures that assaulted you in the arriving process, a chance to finally be emotionally liberated from the tensions of the struggle. You are free to breathe the heavy air of victory and sense the enormous joy of accomplishment! Now is the time to think and to make great decisions!

Hatch out your best ideas and formulate your most audacious and daring plans as you *nest on the crest!*

II. LOOK DOWN

As soon as you arrive, make sure you are standing on solid ground. Then look down! Look for others who are still climbing and struggling. *We are allowed in the Providence of God to succeed not for selfish reasons but for unselfish purposes.* There will be no lasting self-esteem produced by your successes unless you are dedicated to helping your neighbor.

The only joy of success is to know that you've increased your power and capacity to help others. Looking down the mountain, you can see to say, "Look! he's heading the wrong way!" "See! she's taking the wrong turn! She's headed toward a precipice!" "Oh! they are moving too slow; they'll be caught in a storm before they reach base camp. They must move faster." "Look out! they are moving too fast. The road ahead has loose rocks. They must move slowly, cautiously."

You've traveled the road, you've made the climb, you've had your near misses, your risks, your almost falls. Now you can be helpful to those who are still struggling to move up the mountain. The joy of being at the top of the mountain is the joy of reaching down to help others see and develop their possibilities.

Another exciting reward that comes from being high enough to *look down* is that you also enjoy the best perspective to *look beyond!*

III. LOOK BEYOND

If you *nest on the crest,* you will establish new dreams, set new goals, see new visions! And the most viable and authentic principle for goal setting is to *let your goals rise out of human problems that beg for solutions.* When you look beyond and set new goals for your tomorrows, you must also continue to look down. You choose the peaks of future accomplishments by looking at persons who desperately need help!

Guy Vander Jagt, a congressman from Michigan, said, "It's terrible to run out of mountains to climb." Not having goals beyond your goals is more crippling than not reaching your goals! Or, as Viktor Frankl put it, "This *is* must never catch up with the *ought*." You must look beyond! You must continue to exercise the Peak to Peek Principle!

You may be tempted to retire, relax, and spend the rest of your time enjoying your victory and accomplishment. You resist the thought of running into any more of those daring, fearful ventures. But you are to *nest* on the crest, not *roost*! Roosting is sleeping, getting fat, and saying, "I have success," "I have fortune," "I received the promotion," "I have my degree," or "I landed the job." Nesting is hatching out ideas for greater means of serving people. That feeds your self-esteem. And self-esteem will not last more than a day. It will grow stale. You cannot live on yesterday's laurels or yesterday's awards. Fame is fleeting. Fortunes can be quickly dissipated, or threatened through the shifting sands of uncertain and unstable financial developments, nationally and internationally as well as privately. The only safe way to continue to meet your legitimate ego needs is to offer yourself as a channel for good.

And that means *looking beyond!*

The biggest price of success is stewardship in leadership. You will now learn what arriving at the top really costs! Did you think the price of success was buying the ropes to climb and making the hard struggle to finish? That was only the initial investment—the small price.

The price of arriving is satisfying society's demand that you now fill your role as a leader. Others, who still haven't made it to the top, are expecting leadership from you. The person who reaches the peak is now a leader. So if you were concerned about the price to climb to the top or the cost of energy, reserve, and resources just to make the peak, be prepared for the premium payment that you will have to make when you reach success!

Once again, the price of success is stewardship. You must be willing to care and share, to teach and reach, to give others a lift! You are in a position to see possibilities beyond. You can see the problems that lie ahead. This is what a leader does. He sees the possibilities as well as the problems beyond and is responsible for envisioning solutions and communicating them to all who are still following on the road. You are the advance man. You are the head scout. It is never easy or cheap for a leader to fill this role!

What do you do at the top of a mountain? What's the purpose of a peak experience? The purpose is for God to prepare you to be the leader that He wants you to be. You are the center of a circle of influence. There are people around you whose lives depend upon your influence, your example, and your inspiration. Success is unselfish. Failure is selfish. You must succeed, because if you fail, someone else will surely get hurt.

If you live by the Peak to Peek Principle, you'll never be bored. You'll have dreams for tomorrow. Your vision, or peak, will not only keep your own self-esteem alive and thriving until the end of your life but will be an inspiration that will save others somewhere along the line.

What do you do on the top of a mountain? Why, you nest on the crest. You don't lay an egg—you hatch out your biggest project ever.

chapter fourteen

Don't Stop at the Top

THERE IS AN OLD CEMETERY in Switzerland where many of the great mountain climbers are buried. Some of the epitaphs are most appropriate, but there is one that stands out. One of the great mountain climbers died while trying to conquer a rugged peak many years ago. Three words are carved into the tombstone beneath his name: "He died climbing!" I love that! That's what God would like to put as the final sentence of your life and mine! "He didn't die luxuriating." "He didn't die hibernating." "He didn't die procrastinating." "He didn't die vegetating." "He *died climbing!*" The truth is if he hadn't died climbing, he would have been dead the moment he decided to stop climbing, for you can't stop at the top! The greatest temptation that inevitably attacks the climber is the inclination that is in reality a temptation: To quit when you've had your hit!

When Moses led over four hundred thousand Israelites out of captivity in Egypt, God promised that there would be a special homeland waiting for them if they would only have the faith to keep moving ahead! But Moses had a question: "How will we find the right place?" "I will guide you," God replied. "How will you guide me?" Moses questioned again. "Each day, there will be a cloud moving just ahead of you. And at night there will be a pillar of fire moving through the dark sky." God kept his promise. Moses followed the cloud by day and the pillar of fire by night. The people never caught up with the cloud and they never caught up with the fire. God planned it that way. The Jews were being pulled forward as a carrot attracts a rabbit out of the woods.

What is the profound theological and psychological principle of this story? Never catch up with the cloud. Never catch up with the fire. The tension between the *is* and the *ought* must always be present, or you will begin to die. When you stop striving, you start dying! It's that simple.

To die climbing or to die in dull, dead lethargy. Don't stop at the top! When you stop dreaming, you start dying!

Perhaps you remember the lines in *The Chambered Nautilus*, by Oliver Wendell Holmes:

> Build thee more stately mansions, O my soul,
>   As the swift seasons roll!
>   Leave thy low-vaulted past!
> Let each new temple, nobler than the last,
> Shut thee from heaven with a dome more vast,
>   Till thou at length art free,
> Leaving thine outgrown shell by life's
>   unresting sea!

What does it say? If you want to live all the days of your life, you have to struggle ambitiously! Why, then, do people stop at the top!

First, for some the fulfillment appears adequate, the self-esteem is more than they need. So to contemplate a commitment to another struggle seems unnecessary and overpriced. Wrongly they suspect that they can live for months, years, or for the rest of their lives on the self-esteem of the award, the record, the win, the peak experience! But self-esteem has a short life-span.

One day not long ago, I ran into someone I had known back in my college days. He had graduated at the top of his class. He had been very proud! I was shocked to find out that this person, who had had such a marvelous undergraduate education, never developed himself. In the final analysis, I understood what happened. He had been living on the recognition that he received in college. His problem began when he picked up his diploma. He graduated, but he didn't commence! He stopped. His diploma wasn't a new beginning. It was a graduation, not a commencement. All his talent, training, education, accomplishments, and potential were wasted. He stopped at the top!

The second reason some people stop at the top is that they are frankly threatened by their own achievement. "I think I'll quit while I'm ahead," they surmise. Competing against themselves can be a threatening thought.

I confess that if I have a personally satisfying experience in delivering a speech, my joy is tempered by the threat of having to match that higher standard that I've just set the next time I preach or speak.

Rudyard Kipling wrote: "First prizes don't always go to the strongest and brightest man again and again. The man who wins is the man who is sure that he can." That's why some of the people who accomplish the most are not those who run off with the biggest honors and awards. The prize-winners reached the top and stopped! Now they want to take it easy. They enjoyed their laurels, so why not relax?

A third reason some people stop at the top is that their success mesmerizes them. The light air and the heavy victory hypnotize them.

Some time ago I counseled a young lady who was having all kinds of emotional and self-esteem problems. She was having trouble being accepted by others. After she went through three miserable, painful divorces, she came to me pleading for help. As we talked I asked her, "What has been the most exciting, fulfilling experience you've ever had in your life." Then she came alive! "Oh, it was when I won a beauty contest!" she exclaimed. She told me that she was first of sixteen girls. She had reached the top at eighteen years of age. But then what happened? She stopped at the top! She had a peak experience, but she didn't keep on going! You can't live long on that! Don't stop at the top!

I heard a man give his personal testimony in a religious gathering. He was sharing how faith in God had changed his life twenty-seven years before. That was the extent of his story. To me, it was incredibly boring. If he couldn't tell an exciting experience that he had with God last month, his story is old and nobody wants to hear it. He was like the college graduate who hasn't cracked a book or done any serious study since he picked up his degree.

These people all made one basic mistake. They turned a peak experience into a graduation, when it was meant to be a commencement experience. For dynamic living, every graduation is to be a commencement. The peak must give rise to a peek. Achievement must produce a more challenging vision. Keep your mountaintops up to date!

A fourth reason some people stop at the top is they're wearied by the battle they have fought. They arrive battered, tired, scarred, and hurt. "Why go through that again?" they ask. They just aren't sure the peak is worth the price. They want to stop.

Why go through it again? What is the alternative? To stop and die! For that's precisely what happens. As I've said, when we stop growing we start dying!

When the Israelites were wandering through the wilderness, God not only said He would provide them with the tensions to keep pulling them constantly forward, but He also said, "I will give you food along the way." A mysterious thing happened. The Bible says manna fell from the sky. It would fall in the evening, so when the sun came up they would rise to find the divinely supplied nourishment on the ground. The followers of God would gather the food, eat it, and draw nourishment from it.

Then someone came up with the idea of saving time and energy. They were tired of having to go out every day to gather this manna. So they gathered a number of people together and collected as much of the food as they could possibly gather. They were delighted after storing and stacking it, because they wouldn't have to go out every day in the blistering heat to collect their food. But, the next day, they discovered that manna had a short "shelf life." In fact, it was only good for one day, and then it rotted.

I'm reminded of the time I was on the Chapman College Campus Afloat—a ship that cruised through the Pacific for many weeks. Mrs. Schuller and our two older children, Robert and Sheila, were passengers. We encountered a small problem on that ship. Our children loved dry cereal for breakfast. When we came to the table every morning, they would go for their favorite. But each time they filled their bowls, the children would spot tiny bugs in the bowl. That was quite a shock! They wouldn't touch the cereal after that. One morning, as we all sat together at breakfast the children watched the chef come out with an unopened box of cereal. They watched him carefully as he tore open the carton. Breakfast without bugs, they thought! But as they poured the cold milk over the appetizing sight, they noticed the same small creatures rising to the surface. The truth is the microscopic eggs are contained in all dry foodstuffs sold, and if left on the shelf too long the eggs hatch out. Self-esteem from the last success doesn't last long on the shelf either.

Self-esteem that comes from a peak experience is like dry packaged foods: it has a limited life-span before it becomes worthless. Like manna from heaven, self-esteem cannot be hoarded and used up slowly over a long period of time—it doesn't last long. Decay sets in very quickly. The self-esteem that comes from a peak experience does not last more than a season or so. And if you look back on the laurels, the trophies and awards, the honors, the victories, or the past mountaintops, you will discover they no longer feed you. When you try to draw new self-esteem from these old accomplishments by relating the tales to the younger generation, you can see their eyes turn as they are quickly bored. They don't want to listen, because your story is old and stale.

In one of my books, *Move Ahead with Possibility Thinking*, I was addressing myself to the same basic principle when I wrote: "When growth is prohibited, the seed of death and decay is planted in the institution." Why are there some institutions that have a short life-span, while other ones have a long life-span?

Institutions will begin to die only when they stop listening for the cry in the night and the call for help. Institutions that continually look and listen for people who are hurting and then develop a program to meet that need will not die.

These institutions will not only survive but will expand. Why? Because they are built ultimately on a program to meet people's deepest needs!

Then, where growth-restricting obstacles would threaten, we must either eliminate the growth-restricting obstacles or accept the fact that the seed of death and decay is planted in the institution, for *you don't stop at the top!* You must constantly renew, revise, readjust, and update your personal and institutional goals. Ask yourself, "Are we meeting human needs?" And if the answer is yes, you will keep going from *peak* to *peek*. And every new achievement gives you more confidence so that you can climb a higher mountain. You look for bigger needs and set new programs to unfold in a constantly expanding, dynamic way—helping people.

If you think you can marry, have children, get a good job, save a little money, plan for retirement, and then, at a nice age, wrap everything up to spend the rest of your days in the sunshine, you're being misled. Retirement may seem wonderful when you look ahead, but it won't be when it arrives. You'll soon find out how quickly emptiness sets in, because you just can't stop at the top!

There must be a meaningful struggle all your life or you will die before your time! You start dying when you stop struggling! Why does God give us victories after struggling? Not that we might stop and luxuriate or hibernate or vacillate or procrastinate, but that we might dedicate ourselves to conquering the new valley beyond that we never knew was there before. Don't stop at the top. Keep growing. Keep reaching.

Think of your last peak experience. Are you going to settle for that or are you going to reach out for more and more? The experience gave you some self-esteem, but you can't hold on to it. You can't package it. You can't put it on the shelf and then, when you want it, open the cupboard and pour it out to feast on it again. You'll find out it's not fit to eat anymore. As I've said, self-esteem has a short life-span, and just as soon as your self-esteem goes hungry, you need a new peak experience. You cannot stop at the top. There's no way. You will suffer from emotional starvation.

Stop eating and you die physically. Stop exercising and you die physically. Stop breathing and you die physically. Stop learning and you die intellectually. Stop praying and you die spiritually. Stop struggling and your self-esteem starts dying!

A man I know was laid off from a very important industrial position because they found a younger person, who showed greater promise, to replace him. When probed, this is what actually happened: The older fellow was laid off because he was still trying to ride on the laurels of his past experience. He was too tired, too lazy to keep abreast of the new findings, new research, and then knowledge in his field. He had graduated at the top of his class. He was one of the smartest engineers in his time, but he had allowed himself to stop growing. When that happened, he had begun to die, intellectually and organizationally. There is no gain without pain, no crown without a cross. There is no self-esteem without a new challenge faced and met victoriously.

As I've mentioned, I am a jogger. Once in a while, I think that when I reach sixty-five or seventy I can quit running and enjoy my physical fitness. But I can't. I have to keep running until I'm one hundred! I plan on jogging on my one hundredth birthday!

As soon as you quit, you start dying! It's a principle of life. As soon as you quit taking God's challenges to struggle up that next mountain, no matter how old you are you're dying. If you're too tired to climb any more mountains and want to accept the fact that you're going to stop at the top, then plan to dig a hole, for you're dead already.

I was asked recently by an interviewer, "Dr. Schuller,

we understand you've written over a dozen books, your church has over 10,000 members, and your TV program is seen on 150 stations. Isn't it possible that your whole work is turning out to be one big numbers game?" My answer to the question was immediate. "If I were a doctor in charge of inoculating kids in the community, I wouldn't cut notches in my syringe gun and add up how many kids had been vaccinated. I would only look at those who haven't yet been inoculated and immunized. The unfinished task is what sets our challenging goals. We don't stop at the top. We only quit when we've helped everybody that conceivably could be helped in our ministry!"

No person can stop looking for greater mountains to climb so long as he can hear the cries for help coming out of the distant jungle.

You and I cannot stop growing so long as we hear cries in the night. We cannot stop growing so long as we find people who are sick with guilt. We *can* stop growing when the world is made up of perfect people without problems, without heartache and loneliness. Then we can stop! But that will mean we have reached the ultimate top: heaven itself.

Don't stop at the top. Rather, from your new experience gained from your last accomplishment, broaden your base of understanding, awareness, sensitivity to see greater accomplishments. The process of struggle should not leave you with the temptation to retire. But, rather, the successful struggle should inspire you to affirm, "Now I know I can do more than I ever thought possible." "Now I know that I am far more than I ever realized I was." Keep climbing, and at the end of your life what will be said of you?

"He died eating?" No!

"He died sleeping?" No!

"He died looking back and counting his victories?" No!

"He died climbing!" I hope that can be said of me, and I hope it can be said of you!

You cannot stop at the top, or the manna of self-esteem from yesterday's accomplishments will grow stale!

You have to keep running, or you'll lose your physical fitness.

You have to keep studying, or new knowledge will quickly leave your training and past academic degrees worthless.

DON'T STOP AT THE TOP!

You can avoid running, or you can play a
bad fitness game.

You have to start studying, or you can
shortly leave your training and all the same degree
rambles.

DON'T STOP AT THE TOP

chapter fifteen
_____

Speak from the Peak

ONE OF THE GREATEST PROBLEMS facing us today is that
leadership has been surrendered to negative forces.
The blind are leading the blind. The positive-thinking
people are so busy with their exciting ideas, creative
projects, and constructive activity that they don't have
time to make a big scene. It is the losers who are crying
and making the noise!

It seems to work that way in life! How often do you
hear a strong, positive voice like Mary Pruetzel, the
mother of the late Freddy Prinze. Mary, a friend of
mine, spoke out to the world, grief-stricken over her
son's untimely death. She said, "The Lord said to me,
'Stop asking why and start listening.' So I started listening to God and He said to me, 'Freddy was really not
your son, he came into the world through you, and I
gave him to the world through you, but he belonged to
me. Don't cry at your loss. Many women have never
had a child and will never have a child. You had one!
Be thankful for that! You had him for twenty-two
years—be thankful!' "

That is a beautiful story of a positive person addressing herself to the problem of grief. But think for a
moment how most people react. Usually all you hear
are brokenhearted people crying in their self-pity. Crying
in their loss and in their selfish grief.

We are hearing volleys from the valley instead of hearing positive people *speak from the peak!*

There are negative-thinking losers everywhere. And they are very vocal. A particular student was doing poorly in a college class, so he talked to some friends who had taken the same class the semester before. They all agreed that the teacher was boring and showed little interest in the subject being taught. Could it be that this instructor was a person who wasn't able to make it out in the tough, competitive business world, so he found refuge in a classroom as a teacher—with tenure? Here, then, was a loser attempting to teach the younger generation!

Negative thinking has taken over the leadership of many institutions.

It is not unusual to see people with emotional problems studying to be psychiatrists and psychologists. They are afraid of themselves, so they pursue "the study of the mind" hoping to get themselves together and solve their own problems in the process. These people choose careers in accordance with *their needs,* whether it be in teaching, preaching, or psychology. The danger here is that we may have weak people in powerful positions! So we hear them verbalize their problems!

Why don't we hear people *speak from the peak?* Why aren't the winners in command? I talked to the president of a large corporation in New York City. "You ought to be a candidate for the presidency of the United States," I said. "You are brilliant! You're a successful administrator and an honest and skillful leader. You have all the qualities of a great President!"

But he is not in government. Why not? Because he is so positive and creative that he is involved in many projects, allowing him no time to get interested in politics!"

I remember being interviewed by a very negative newspaper reporter. After the interview I said, "Now I have a question for you. Why is a bright guy like you so cynical? You seem to doubt everything I say." "Well," he said, "I do nothing but interview people with problems." "I don't have a problem," I commented; "why did you interview me?" "Well," he answered, "you were a special assignment." So I raised this question: "Is it possible that your cynicism is an occupational hazard? And is it possible that you are interpreting the world from your cynical perspective?"

So the cynics are sounding off. We are hearing volleys of folly from the valley, while positive-thinking people who have it all together don't have time to parade, fight, or argue, because they are so busy pursuing their exciting dreams and projects. If we are so busy achieving, succeeding, and watching our dreams come true, we can easily forget to speak from the peak!

Successful achievers have a responsibility for leadership in the world. We cannot surrender leadership to loud losers. Leadership must not be surrendered to the weak. Leadership must come from the peak. The blind are leading the blind. There are losers and negative thinkers teaching our world. That's tragic!

The world must start listening to winners and stop listening to losers.

Don't listen to the volleys from the valleys. If you want to know the truth, listen to positive-thinking people. Accomplished persons must do the talking so that winners are leading the way instead of losers.

Take a good look at our world today. Many people don't believe in the institution of marriage anymore. But look at the people speaking that way! They are the losers, not the winners. Many "anti-family" and "anti-marriage" articles and views are coming from adults who were, as children, emotionally wounded and victimized when their parents split up or fought bitterly. Time and time again I hear men and women say, "I'll have my relationships with the opposite sex, but I won't make any commitment." Why? Because they were hurt when their partner cheated on them and left the nest! So they become anti-marriage exponents. Their voices are volleys from the valleys. We must hear people speak from the peak!

I want to say a good word for marriage! I have been married to my first and only wife for nearly twenty-seven years, and there is nothing greater than having a relationship in which two people have unconditional commitments to care about each other until the end! You can't beat that! We have five beautiful children who have all grown up in our home. The family is a great institution! It's the only place where people care about each other, support each other, pray for each other, and give to each other without keeping score! You are not listening to a loser! You're listening to a winner! I speak from the peak!

What is the fee of success, the price tag of achievement? *"Unto whom much is given, much will be required."* Look at all the corruption in the world. Somebody needs to counteract all those negative ideas and that somebody must be you!

Stop being silent! When you hear loud negative voices, put a smile on your face and speak out! Tell them the truth! Tell them they have only two choices: to be negative or to be positive, to be a cynic or to be a believer, to love or to have hostility, to make commitments or to play it loose. The only choice that produces any lasting hope, love, and peace is in the relationship with God, your creator. He has done a lot for you, hasn't He? *Speak from the peak!*

In my book *You Can Become the Person You Want to Be,* I tell the story of a school in South Dakota where some of the pupils are Down's-Syndrome children (unable to read and write). In my book, I shared the way these children were learning to read and write whole sentences. Then I received a very negative letter from a colleague concerning this school. Later I discovered that this man had a Down's-Syndrome child and he and his wife were told that they should institutionalize him. They were told that he was hopeless—incapable of learning. They put the child in an institution and accepted the fact that their child was a hopeless case. When my book came out, their child was twenty-one years old and could not even read the word EXIT. They read my book and became bitter when they read that there are Down's-Syndrome children learning to read whole sentences. They had listened to losers! If you've been listening to losers, you'll probably be angry if a winner starts talking, because it may be a judgment upon what you have been doing.

Losers get angry with winners! Negative people can't stand positive people! Negativity cannot stand positiveness!

Desperate negative people will try to slaughter the integrity of the positive thinker by calling him a Pollyanna phony!

Somebody might say, "Are you saying that we should never sound off when we're negative?" And my answer is "Never verbalize a negative emotion unless you are prepared to insulate vulnerable minds from the danger of being programmed or infected by negative thoughts that can become self-fulfilling prophecies."

All ideas can have within themselves the possibility of becoming a reality.

An idea contains within itself the power to actualize itself. If a wife asks her husband, "Are you cheating on me?" and if she constantly nags him, insisting that he is unfaithful, in time he will cheat on her. It happens again and again. Never verbalize a negative emotion unless you know that you have shielded those vulnerable minds.

How can you attack a negative situation safely without infecting people with the urge to negative action that they hadn't really thought about? *Never speak out on a negative problem unless you have a positive idea to sell that will by indirection correct the problem!*

Do not spout off your frustrations, no matter how valid they may be. The only thing you should do is come up with a better idea—a problem-correcting dream! Now sell the idea! When people buy the idea, they may not even be aware that they are solving a problem!

How do you speak from the peak? You speak *positively*, not negatively. You give an idea or a dream that corrects the problem. You are sane, not insane! Why do I say that?

The Man of La Mancha, Don Quixote, only looks at the good. He's not unaware of the bad, but he doesn't talk about it. He talks about good and ignores the evil. If he keeps talking about the good, then people will become good. And if they become good, the bad will be self-correcting! He has the positive approach.

In the stage play *Man of La Mancha*, what happened to Don Quixote? He was accused of being crazy. Who's crazy? the Man of La Mancha asks. Am I crazy because I see the world as it could become? Or is the world crazy because it sees itself as it is?

I have thought about that question for twelve years, ever since I saw the play, and I now know the answer. Who's crazy? The man who sees the world as it is and paints the picture as it is and reports the news as it is? Or the man who sees it as it could become? Here's the answer. *The man is crazy who fails to lift the rest of the world.* The person who paints only the dark picture spreads sickness, because people believe it. They become depressed and lose their own strength to resist. They join what they consider to be irrevocable forces. (If you can't beat them, join them!)

By contrast, we have the Man of La Mancha, who dreams the impossible, and people call him crazy! (The cynics always call positive thinkers crazy.)

It is the negative person who is crazy, for he sees the world as it is. He tells the world what he sees and puts life down in the process. The only sane person is a positive-thinking person with a redeeming idea. Because he gives the world a star, a dream, and a positive idea. He tells the world, "You are beautiful!"

We tend to become what we expect people to expect us to be!

> Ultimately I am not what I think I am,
> I am not what you think I am,
> I am what what I think you think I am.

Are you a winner? Have you been too busy to speak from the peak? Stop today and speak from the peak. Don't surrender to the loud voices of the losers. Speak up and overpower the sounds of the negative forces.

chapter sixteen

How to Climb Down a Mountain Without Falling

ALLOW ME TO RESTATE what I mean by the "Peak to Peek Principle." A *peak* experience is an experience of success, achievement, and accomplishment which feeds your self-esteem, which then expands your self-confidence. So the *peak* experience gives you a *peek* experience: a vision of greater accomplishments that you can realize in the months and years ahead!

You need to know that you are a worthy and beautiful person! A *peak* experience is an accomplishment or an achievement that leaves you with a consciousness that you are more than you ever thought you were.

In developing this book, I would be negligent if I didn't discuss the subject of this chapter: "How to Climb Down a Mountain Without Falling." In other words, when you've had a highly stimulating peak experience and you have to come down, how do you handle it? What happens after you've been the President of the United States? When you've been the chairman of the board and retire and you're no longer in a powerful, decision-making role?

What do you do when the telephone no longer rings for you and people no longer seek your counsel? How do you handle that? Or you've been to the height of fame and fortune and been replaced? What happens when you're fired or retired or simply tired? Or divorced? Or replaced by new and younger climbers?

How do you keep topping the last achievement? When you can't match the stimulation of your peak experience, what then?

For twenty-seven years in my profession I've seen *how* many people handle the experience of coming down from the heights to which they successfully aspired. Some forcibly, because of old age; others because of other circumstances beyond their control; and many just because they are tired of what they call "the rat race." I know what a problem it is for many people. Some are old and are asking, "How can I stay alive in retirement?" How do you climb down a mountain without losing your self-esteem? How can you feel that you are a wonderful, worthy person when you're just one of the masses in the valley?

> Yesterday I was climbing
> Today I am on top
> Tomorrow I must come down

You can come down from the top of the mountain and have your self-esteem fulfilled if you have three things: (1) A purpose to live for. (2) A self that you can live with. (3) A faith that you can live by.

Chuck Colson was one of the most powerful men in the country. He was special counsel to the President of the United States, until he fell down the mountain—all the way to prison. That's coming down a mountain the hard way! But today he has a more exciting life than ever before, because he has found a purpose to live for: to spread God's love to prisoners all over America.

In Chuck's own words, "I suppose my life is a paradox in that all those years that I was striving to achieve power, success, wealth, and prominence by the world's standards, I had to come to that one point where I realized how empty and meaningless life was!

"I once thought, when I had all the powers that man can confer upon man, when my office was next to the President of the United States, when I could fly on Air Force One, and when I could write executive orders, that I really knew what manpower was. And that's all pretense. If we think by building marble and glass temples of power in Washington that we can solve the problem of the human heart, we cannot! Because the sickness which is affecting mankind today is alienation: one person set against another, nations set against one another, races divided, families divided, divorces outpacing marriages.

"It wasn't until I fell and reached bottom that I found life through finding a faith in God.

"My wife and I often sit at the breakfast table reading stacks of letters that have come in from people who are responding to my book *Born Again*, the story of what God has done in my life, and Patty and I weep as we read about lives being changed!

"A young graduate student wrote that he was contemplating suicide until he read my book, and instead of taking his life he gave his life to Christ! Now he's working, is married, and has a lovely family. And I hear from families who are reconciled, or couples broken up who, through the power of Christ, come together. I have to admit that the tough ex-marine captain, the White House hatchet man (so they called me) weeps with joy and thanksgiving to God that he changed my life and has called me to a special service.

"God has called me into the prisons, and I go to them all across America. My colleagues and I invite inmates to live with us for two weeks in Washington, D.C. And they come to know what the beauty of fellowship is— being together with brothers and sisters who really love them. They come to know the reconciling power of God's love. Then they go back into the prisons to finish their sentences, and God's love is being shared in those horrible, cold, dank, dark concrete holes known as prisons, rehabilitating men where government and the prison system have failed."

Like Chuck Colson, you can *climb* down the mountain without falling, if you have *a purpose to live for*. But you need something else, too: *a self that you can live with!*

Eldridge Cleaver reached a mountaintop and he climbed down without falling. Eldridge Cleaver knew what it was like to be at the top of a mountain only to come down. At one time he was the Peace and Freedom Party candidate for the presidency of the United States. He was by his own confession a Communist! And when he went to Cuba and North Vietnam, he was treated like a king—the red carpet was rolled out. He had a luxurious apartment in Paris and another on the Mediterranean. He had it made!

But Eldridge Cleaver was running! Running from a self that had been stung and hurt by radical prejudice in youth. He ran into a reactionary, negative, and violent activity. He kept running until one day he stopped and cried out to God. He was tired of running! Then God came into his life and turned him around. Eldridge Cleaver became a new self!

In Eldridge Cleaver's own words:

"You talk about falling from peaks? Well, you don't have to be a member of the White House staff, or a hatchet man for the President in order to be on a peak. But you can be a hatchet man for other causes, and even a good cause can be distorted and turned into a bad cause because of the way you go about it! Be careful!

"I found myself on a peak and then I found myself at the bottom.

"When I look back at my life, trying to understand how my life turned, I see that it was one exclusion after another.

"It's fantastic to see that I've gone back to being twelve years old, when I stopped listening to my mother. I couldn't stand to hear her, because she was always trying to show me a point.

"Recently Mom, who is sixty-nine now, said, 'Up until the time you were twelve years old, you were a little angel. But when you turned twelve you turned into a little devil. And the whole process of you going away and turning your back on the family and dropping out of one thing and then another.'

"Leaving my family, my circle of friends that I grew up with, and quitting my high school football team. Eventually I was excluded from the normal and broad movement of black people, in the civil rights movement, and got hung up in the very fringe element of the Black Panther Party.

"There was a time when I took pride in being on the FBI's 'most wanted' list, and that's the truth! But, ultimately, I was excluded from the party and the U.S. itself! Then I found myself absolutely alone, without any idea of myself, of how to get back, of how to come out of that dead end and how to be reunited with people and friends, not to mention coming back home!

"It was only after experiencing that total isolation and exclusion that I was able to be open to receiving faith. I discovered doors opening and a process of inclusion beginning: The pendulum began to swing the other way! A process of reconciliation began that could not have possibly come about any other way! I found myself, first of all, included and reconciled with my pursuers. The first step back was to be reunited with the FBI, who was after me, and finally to come back to the country and be reunited with family and old friends who had first scorned me with my return.

"There's a process of healing taking place, and it's wonderful to be able to see how the healing power of love can build bridges between people, overcome generation gaps, racial divides, and class divisions. I experienced the power to break out of isolation.

"I can see myself on the road to that ultimate inclusion at the end of this earthly life, when I'll be reunited with the Heavenly Father! I praise God that those things are possible and I can smile again because I have a smile inside and outside."

Eldridge Cleaver climbed down his mountain by falling into faith and discovered a self he can live with.

He has stopped running—he likes himself! He's a new man!

You can climb down a mountain without falling. You'll rise higher than ever before *if you have a purpose that you can live for, a self that you can live with,* and *a faith that you can live by*.

There is no one person who so vividly portrays a faith

to live by than my dear friend Corrie ten Boom, now eighty-six years old.

Corrie was on top of the mountain—in her forties. She had everything going for her in Holland. A loving father, a beautiful sister, and a successful trade. But then Hitler moved in and began killing the Jews, and as faithful Christians, they did everything they could to save their Jewish friends. They built a secret room in the back of their house and hid the Jews so they could get them out of the country. She and her family risked their lives to help the Jews.

Then, one morning, Gestapo agents stormed into their home and demanded to know where the Jews were hidden. Corrie, Betsie (her sister), and her father were caught red-handed. They were forcibly taken from their home and sent to a concentration camp, where she lost her sister. In her book *The Hiding Place*, Corrie tells only of the miracle way in which she was released. *A faith to live by*—Corrie knows!

Corrie knew what it was like to come down from youth to old age, from a loving family to loneliness. But she had a faith to live by. What vitality and enthusiasm she has too! And today, in her eighties, she is writing books.

In Corrie's own words:

"I'm glad that I can tell a little about that faith—I have several chapters of my life that I'd like to share with you.

"First, I was in a happy home with Father and Betsie, my sister. I had a good watchmaking business and I was the first licensed woman watchmaker. Then came that terrible time when I had to be in prison. Then I had a chapter in which I was a tramp for the Lord—thirty-three years! And now, this is a new chapter: I am now an alien resident of America and I can stay here and write my books! I am happy for that, because now I am no longer a tramp! The Lord has given me a house!

"Oh, you might think I'm retiring. Not at all. You call it retirement, I just say I have new tires!

"When I was in that terrible camp, where ninety-five thousand women were killed or died, my sister included, I learned that when you have Jesus Christ, you possess divine power that silences the enemy and inflicts upon him the danger he would inflict upon you. That is faith in Jesus Christ.

"He makes us more than conquerors! Yes, He is the victory that overcomes the world! And He gives you not a spirit of fear but the spirit of power and of love and of a sound mind.

"People say that I have a great faith. Perhaps some of you say my faith is not so great.

"God can make you victorious, and it doesn't matter if our faith is small if there's only faith in that great God.

"If it's as small as a mustard seed it is sufficient to remove mountains."

Yes, Jesus is the same
yesterday when I was climbing,
today when I stood on the peak,
and forever—even if I must come down!

chapter seventeen

The Heartbeat of a Great Climber

WHAT'S THE HEARTBEAT of a climber really like? Before I answer that question, allow me to make three very important statements:

First, God wants you to have a great life.

Second, having a great life is enjoying the pride of accomplishment.

Third, there can be no pride of accomplishment without conquering a mountain. God wants you to have the greatest feeling in the world: the joy of self-esteem that comes when you fulfill the challenges that God puts before you. So God calls us to be climbers.

There are two kinds of people who avoid mountain climbing. One is the coasters. These people just drift along and hope that something's going to happen—maybe they'll have a lucky break and become successful. Somebody said, "Even a dead fish can float downstream." There are a lot of people that take that attitude toward life. No dreams, no commitments, no goals, no plans. They just coast along and wonder why they don't have real excitement in life.

The second kind of people are those who cut out. They are the people who just don't want to be on planet earth. They want out of the rat race. The whole thought of achievement and motivation is just too much. They don't care, so they deliberately choose not to develop themselves. As a result, they don't grow.

They are like the fellow whose supervisor told him to load some heavy boxes on a truck. It was hot and humid and near the end of the day. "I can't lift those boxes," he complained. "My bursitis is bothering me again." "That's too bad," his boss lamented. "When your bursitis doesn't bother you, how high can you reach?" "Oh, I can reach . . ." and he raised his arm high into the air! He was trying to cut out.

Earlier, I mentioned Abraham Maslow and his concept of the Jonah complex. Maslow refers to the evasion of growth, even though all would like to be better than they are. All of us have an impulse to improve ourselves toward actualizing our potential. So then, what causes people to coast or to cut out? It is the fear of our own greatness—an evasion of our destiny. We run away from our best opportunities.

God calls every one of us to be climbers, not coasters or people who cut out. In order to be a climber, you must have the heart of a climber. What does that mean? It means that God gives you a call, a conscience, and courage.

I. A CALL

A climber is somebody who has a heart, hears a call, and is driven by a sense of destiny. He must do it!

When I used to read and hear stories about mountain climbers, I'd think: What a crazy thing to do. Who in the world would want to spend his time, money, and energy climbing a mountain and risking his precious life?

Then I talked to some mountain climbers at Katmandu. They were preparing to scale Mount Everest, so I asked them why they wanted to climb a mountain. And they all said that they were driven by a destiny. They had to do it. It was in their blood. And that same principle holds true in your life and in mine. When you discover God's plan and purpose for you, you have a sense of destiny. God has a plan for every person. God has a purpose for everything!

On a plane from Los Angeles to New York, the man

next to me turned and said, "What do you do?" "Guess," I enthused. And it turned into a guessing game as he named off several professions. He never did guess, so I finally told him. "I am a minister." "Oh," he said, "I am a believer." "What does that mean to you?" I prodded. "I believe there's a purpose for everybody and a purpose for everything," he explained. "So do I!" I exclaimed.

Then he followed with a puzzling question, "What is the purpose of a mouse?" I hadn't the foggiest idea. He had caught me off guard. "Well," I responded, "I never really thought about it. What is the purpose of a mouse?" "It's good for business," he answered. Then he rattled off how much money is generated in the gross national product by the existence of mice. Mousetraps, cat food and veterinarian costs, to name a few. "That's just the beginning!" he announced.

Who would have thought of the opportunities created because of mice? I never realized thousands of people would be out of work if there were no mice. By the time he finished talking, I was really impressed and felt thankful to God for all those mice! If there's a purpose for mice, then there must be a purpose for you and for me.

God is going to give you a problem, and that will be your opportunity. He will give you challenges. That will be your mountain. That is God's greatest gift to you. Face your mountains instead of cutting out or coasting. You'll experience the greatest joy of life: the joy of self-esteem that comes when you know you did what you had to do.

People used to ask me if I had a call to my profession as a minister. "What do you mean, 'a call'?" I'd ask. I knew what they meant after they began to explain it, and I would say, "Sure, I have that!" I have something inside of me that says that's what I have to do. That's what I have to be. That's my reason for being born. That's my only reason for taking up space on planet earth. That's why God put me here.

A church leader once commented to a talented young fellow, "I think you should have a call to become a pastor." "But I don't feel the call," the boy answered. "Maybe you're not in calling distance," the pastor replied. "Get close to God and you'll get a call!"

You'll find out what mountain He wants you to climb!

II. A CAUSE

Oftentimes, the place to find your call is the biggest problem that you face.

Mountain climbers are part of a great cause. They see that this calling is all-important because it's locked into a cause that has tremendous significance. I was talking with a friend whom I converse with every other week. This man had one of the highest positions of power in the government of the United States until the change in administration. Now he's among the ranks of the unemployed. "How are you doing?" I asked him. "Bob," he said, "I need a great cause!"

I told my friend that a call must have integrity, and in order to have integrity it has to help people who are hurting. A call to a great cause must do that.

The heartbeat of a climber is driven by a call to a great cause. It will take the form of a dream. And when it does, in front of you will be a mountain. Big! Almost humanly impossible, but you will not be intimidated by impossibilities. The call will grip you and it will grab you!

III. CONSCIENCE

The third thing you'll have after a call to a great cause is a conscience. The conscience will not let you turn back from your opportunity.

Born and raised on an Iowa farm, I learned the importance of carrying my own weight! I'm from a large family, and all of us had chores to do! Some had to load hay, others had to milk cows, while the little ones gathered eggs. Each of us had our chores to do, and there were no excuses. If it was raining or snowing, we simply bundled up and went out. We had no running water, so we carried the water in pails. Sometimes it would freeze and cling to the sides of the bucket before we even reached the house. I'll never forget those cold days. Nobody said, "You poor little child, you're going to freeze!" We were taught to be tough!

Once in a while I would come crying into the house, but my stern father would say in no uncertain terms, "Just because you've got a problem doesn't give you an excuse!" I learned from the beginning that you don't make excuses out of problems. Possibility thinkers don't turn problems into excuses for quitting.

A conscience was developed as far as responsibility is concerned. I could not have fulfilled my responsibility as a church leader if I hadn't developed a tremendous sense of conscience over ideas that came from God. When you get a call to a great cause, your conscience will not let you turn your back on it.

IV. COURAGE

A friend asked me, "Twenty-five years ago, when you were holding worship services in the drive-in theater, did you ever dream of this church you have now?"

"I remember when this dream first emerged, and it was so big," I said. "We had 150 members when the dream came: the church, with fountains and everything!" It was so exciting! I thought it would be so beautiful! But I lacked one thing. I had the call and the conscience, but I didn't have the courage.

That same summer, Norman Vincent Peale asked if I'd preach for him at the prestigious Marble Collegiate Church, on Fifth Avenue, so I flew to New York. In Norman's office was a calender that read: *"I'd rather do something great and fail than attempt to do nothing and succeed!"* God used that slogan to give me the courage I needed for my work.

If there was no possibility of failure, then victory would be meaningless. If there was no possibility of defeat, then the accomplishment would be hollow. And that's why there's no self-esteem without a struggle. There's no salvation without a sacrifice. There's no crown without a cross.

You need courage, too. You need it for your dream.

When you have a calling, a great cause to work for, you need a conscience that will not let you quit. You also need courage. The courage to risk failure, to risk criticism, or to face mockery. Courage to face the put-downs of other people! There's an enormous power of good in this world, and it ultimately comes from the hearts of those who are the instruments of God. They are the minds through which God is thinking. They are the hearts through which God is loving. They are the hands through which God is helping. They are the voices through which God is speaking.

We need climbers. People who look for a problem, solve it, and end up with the greatest joy. The joy of self-respect. The joy of having a peak experience: a mountaintop experience that leaves you with a tremendous sense of self-affirmation or, in the words of Abraham Maslow, a self-actualizing encounter.

A good friend of mine, Ralph Showers, had an inner call to build a ranch for mentally retarded adults so they could be taught to have meaningful jobs and have tremendous self-esteem. He had no money, but he had a call! He had a conscience. He couldn't turn his back on the idea. It would have haunted him all his life. So he was driven by a call and a conscience. He had courage. Today, in Arizona, a ranch for the mentally retarded brings tremendous joy to many young adults.

Real courage. Intestinal strength. Inner strength. The Bible uses the word *bowels*—the innards. The deepest part of you. You must have nerve. Mountain climbers have it. They are willing to take risks. They know they'd rather die trying to do something than live turning their back on God's call.

There are millions of people who have sold their minds and hearts out to all sorts of negative thinking. They put down people who have dreams. They put down people who have high hopes. They squelch enthusiasm and try to defeat the dreamers. If you want to be a climber, you have to have the courage to face that kind of crowd. Don't let them get under your skin. Just keep going—climb your mountain!

The heart of a climber is driven by a call. He's driven to seek a great cause. He's driven by a conscience to be faithful to that call. And he's driven by a courage to climb even if he has to die doing it. God can make you a climber. Look beyond yourself. You are surrounded by people who have negative thoughts. No enthusiasm for life. You have something they need.

If you want to know what kind of person a climber is, look at Jesus Christ. He was the greatest mountain climber of all times. He climbed all the way to the top of the mountain of Calvary. And from that point He has been conquering the hearts of men and women for two thousand years. From His mountain peak, Jesus Christ won my heart.

But Jesus didn't have to climb that mountain—He could have stopped before He reached the top. Praying in the Garden of Gethsemane, Jesus said, "Father, Father, everything is possible for you. Take away this cup from me. Yet I want your will, not mine." (Mark 14:36) He could have escaped the mob that arrested Him, but He didn't. He wasn't martyred, tricked, or cornered. He willingly sacrificed His life, for it was all part of the plan. Jesus knew what He had to do, and with joy He set His face to the cross!

A call—a great cause, a conscience, and courage. Start climbing! *In a world with so many problems, there are so many mountains to climb! Be a climber!*

chapter eighteen

How to Have a Peak Experience

HOW CAN YOU HAVE A PEAK EXPERIENCE in life? How can you rise to the top of a mountain?

"Where there is no vision, the people perish"

I

A *peak* experience is an experience that leaves you with an awareness that you are more than you thought you were. It is a self-affirming, positive experience that builds your self-esteem! And *peak* experiences give you a *peek* (or vision expanding) experience of what you can amount to.

You need to have a peek into the future in order to have hope for today. When you see possibilities in the path ahead, you're inspired with energy and enthusiasm for living. Now, unless you have a peek into the future you can never expect to rise to other mountain peaks of achievement and accomplishment. That's the Peak to Peek Principle, and it ties together the very vitality and zest of real living.

A man selling balloons on the streets of New York City knew how to attract a crowd before he offered his wares for sale. He took a white balloon, filled it with helium, and let it float upward. Next he filled a red balloon and released it. Then he added a yellow one. As the red, yellow, and white balloons floated above his head, the little children gathered around to buy his balloons. A hesitant black boy looked up at the balloons and finally asked, "If you filled a black balloon, would it go up too?" The man looked down and said, "Why, sure, it's not the color of the balloon, it's what's inside that makes it go up."

A *peak* experience is not dependent on the color of your skin or whether you are male or female. Nor is it your physical construction that makes a mountaintop experience possible. *What's inside of you* determines whether you achieve peak experiences in your life. Climbing to the peak of a mountain depends upon your mind and your attitudes.

I find it fascinating to read the stories, many of them legendary, about the late Houdini. That masterful magician was probably a better locksmith than he was a magician. He had a standing challenge that he could get out of any locked jail in sixty minutes, providing they would let him enter in his regular street clothes and not watch him work.

One of the stories is about a little town in the British Isles that decided to challenge and perhaps embarrass the great Houdini. This town had just completed an escape-proof jail, and they invited Houdini to see if he could break out.

He accepted the challenge and was allowed to enter the jail in his street clothes. People said they saw the local locksmith turn the lock some strange way, and then, with the clang of steel, the spectators turned their backs and left Houdini alone to work. He had hidden a long, flexible steel rod in his belt, which is what he used to try to trip the lock. He worked for thirty minutes. He kept his ear close to the lock . . . forty-five minutes, and then an hour passed, and he was perspiring. After two hours, he was exhausted. He leaned against the door, and to his amazement, it fell open. The locksmith had not locked the door! It was a trick on the great escape artist.

The door was locked only in Houdini's mind.

Some of you think that you can't climb that mountain

peak. *The only place where it is impossible is in your thinking.* That's the only place that's locked!

What inner qualities of mind make peak experiences possible? I can answer that all-important, key question in five words, and they all rhyme.

To climb the mountain you need a *dream*. Then you have to put a *gleam* on your dream. Then you need a *scheme* to back up your dream. Then put a *beam* under your dream. Finally, you need a *team* to build the dream that leads to the mountaintop.

So, first, you need a *dream*. Nobody climbs a mountain unless he has a burning desire to climb it. Nothing is as powerful as a dream that consumes you to the point that you are willing to die for it.

I've never been a mountain climber, but I remember talking to those mountain climbers in Katmandu. Now, Katmandu is at the base of the Himalaya Moutains, and that's the closest I've ever gotten to Mount Everest. As I was passing through the airport, I stopped to talk with some people who were about to climb Mount Everest. You could see fire in their eyes! They didn't care if they got killed climbing the mountain. They had a dream, a powerful dream. Peak experiences begin with *such* a dream!

When I saw the vision of what God could do through the Crystal Cathedral, I said I would gladly shorten my life by twenty years if that's what it required to build this Cathedral to the glory of God. Nobody has a peak experience unless it begins with a dream that consumes the dreamer to the point that it means more than life itself.

What do I mean by a dream? I mean a vision that comes from God Himself. I have no doubt that God has a plan for every life and He has a plan for you.

"I have a plan for your life; it is a plan for your good and not evil; it is a plan to give you a future and a hope."
(Jeremiah 29:11)

You didn't ask to be born—you weren't your own idea. No human being ever had the chance to decide whether to be born or not. You were God's idea. Therefore it makes sense to go back to the God who conceived of your conception as a person. Ask Him, "Lord, what was your plan for me? What do you want me to do with my life?"

It's amazing how many people fail because they ignore the inventor and dream up their own ideas: What would I like to do? What would be most profitable? Then they make decisions and start off expecting everybody else to support them!

We have all read stories of explorers who took cameras and recording equipment into primitive areas only to have them destroyed by the natives. Threatened by the unfamiliar equipment, these natives became frightened. They didn't understand the purpose of the invention or of the inventor.

God created you and allowed you to be born because he wants to see you where you are. He is the inventor, and He has a specific purpose for each of His inventions— for you and me. He wants to do something beautiful with your life.

Begin your dream by making a commitment of your life to God—your creator.

II

The second thing you need is to put a *gleam* on the dream. What do I mean by a gleam? I mean the kind of sparkle that turns a dream into a diamond—an idea into a gem! This happens when you take the dream and add the quality of excellence—do it just a little better than anybody else. In everything you do, try to do it better. than you did the last time. Compete against yourself; then you compete against the experts!

I said to somebody who was admiring the Crystal Cathedral that seldom is an idea born that has within itself the potential for excellence, and more rarely is such an idea allowed to develop to its full blossom without yielding to pressures of mediocrity. Philip Johnson, the architect of the Crystal Cathedral, told me a favorite saying of one of his partners, the late Mies van der Rohe: "God is in the details." This means a great deal when you talk about design and architecture. It means a great deal when you talk about dreams that need gleams to make them sparkle. Make the details exquisite!

The compulsion to excellence. What is it? I know what it is for me. I believe that the dream comes from God. We are not the owners of our dream; we are only the stewards of the idea. It is our responsibility to take that idea from God and develop it to its full potential until an accomplished achievement is handed back to a Holy God, without spot, wrinkle, or blemish. That's the drive for excellence. And when you put the gleam of excellence on your dream, great power is unleashed.

Beyond excellence is the gleaming quality that we call "ministry." Our dreams must help people who are hurting. I lecture frequently at the University of California Graduate School of Business Managment. I have had in my seminars some of the most powerful chief executive officers, of some of the largest corporations on the Pacific coast. I've posed the questions "Where do goals arise? How many goals in businesses and corporations rise out of the ego needs of the power-centered person?"

We must be careful that goals don't rise out of unfulfilled ego needs of the power-centered person in the institution! This happens too often. Every person has his or her ego needs. What is important is that we understand that we have these ego needs and understand how they can be fulfilled. We must be careful that the goals of the institution that we set are not rising out of our own unfulfilled ego needs. Otherwise, we can be sure that we are on a collision course with ultimate failure.

Dynamic goals must always rise out of authentic needs. They must help people who are hurting. That's what will keep you from quitting. Some friends of mine with their own business have almost a thousand employees on their payroll. They said to me one day, "We're rich enough now so that we could retire and live comfortably all our lives. We've thought about it, but we can't. We have one thousand people whose jobs depend on us. If we quit, they're unemployed." That's what drives them. That's the gleam on their dream.

I know of a retail shopping center that had problems from the day it opened, for a simple reason. The power people planned what they thought would be a spectacular center, but they built it in a community that didn't need it. The power source never bothered to research the area to find out the needs of the people. Now they can't understand why the community doesn't support them!

The same thing happened with the new supersonic airplane the Concorde. I have a friend who is involved in the Concorde controversy. He tells me that the Concorde is a failure and will be a failure because the manufacturers in France and England are not able to sell the plane to the major airlines in the United States. The conflict has increased, and the United States shows little interest in purchasing the aircraft. One of the executive officers on the West Coast said: "Look, don't blame us for not buying your plane. You never asked us what kind of a plane we wanted. If you had asked us we would have given you some guidelines. For instance: It has to fly 1400 miles an hour, carry 200 paying passengers, and can't consume more than so much fuel. But you sat in your towers in London and Paris and designed it without any input from other major airline executives."

To put a gleam on your dream, ask these three important questions: Would it be a great thing for God? Would it help people who are hurting? Would it be a great thing for our country and our community and our world?

With a yes answer, you are on your way to a peak experience.

III

Have a dream . . . put a gleam on that dream . . . then develop a *scheme* to back it up.

The first dream I ever had came to me when I was a little boy, and I began to scheme how I could accomplish it. I had the dream that I wanted to be a minister. And then I had to develop the scheme—it meant eight years of school, four years of high school, four years in college, and then three years in theological graduate school. That's nineteen years of education. At the age of five, I made that commitment.

Anything can be accomplished if you're willing to pay the price, prepare for it, and stick with the scheme. The scheme: How much will it take? What will it cost? What kind of resources will I need? What kind of help will I need?

IV

A dream, a gleam, a scheme, and then you need a *beam* under the dream! A beam to keep the roof from falling in and the whole thing from coming apart. You have the God-inspired *dream*. You've got the divine *scheme* as to how it can happen, given enough time and resources. Now what you need is the beam under the dream. The beam is the spiritual power to keep yourself from quitting when negative forces attack you.

Every time you have a dream, you can expect negative forces to move in, because *every time you set a new goal, you establish a new area of conflict*. That's a principle! Negative forces will be released.

You must prepare for this. In building a cave, as soon as you construct an entrance, you put in some beams so it won't collapse. As you keep building the cave larger and larger, you put in more supportive beams.

What are the beams that keep your dreams alive? I'll tell you one of my beams. It's what I call two-way prayer. I couldn't possibly succeed at any of my dreams without God, because He alone can make it happen successfully. That means that God and I had better be on the best of terms. We have to communicate moment by moment.

What is this prayer form? I imagine a little window at the top of my head. You know the cars that have sun roofs? Well, I imagine the top of my head like one of the cars with sun roofs. The sun roof is pulled back and the window is open. I'm constantly waiting for God's sunlight of wisdom to fall in and shape my thinking, mold my behavior, and control my feelings. That's constant prayer life.

You've got a dream, and there's a gleam on the dream. There's a scheme to make the dream come true. You're building beams under your dreams. Now what do you need?

V

You now need a *team* to build it! You can't build your dream alone, I can't build my dream alone. No businessman builds his dream—the customers build it. No politician builds his dream—only those who vote for him make it come true.

"No man is an island"—no man stands alone.

I shall never forget the time, on a ship sailing to the South Seas, when the captain said that on the next day the ship would go through a very narrow passage in the Coral Sea. When we were told the ship was approaching this point, all the passengers got on deck. The ship needed thirty feet of water to avoid grounding. In the shallow coral regions we were passing through, there was only one place where the water was deeper than thirty feet, and this passageway was so narrow I had the impression that it was hardly wide enough for our ship. To maneuver such a huge ship through such a narrow crevice was indeed precarious.

As we came closer, the captain cut the forward speed. Off in the distance, we saw a little motorboat coming toward us, leaving its wide, white wake. In that motorboat was a special navigator from Australia. He stepped onto our ship through a little hole down below. You could see him come in. He came up the elevator, and the captain of our ship saluted him and stepped aside. Then this expert navigator from Australia took the helm. He specialized in taking ships through this narrow passage. That was teamwork.

Do you know who that special pilot is for me? His name is Jesus Christ. I make sure that Jesus Christ is at the helm, and as I go through some narrow waters, I know I'll reach port safely.

I received a letter from a thirty-six-year-old woman who had probably not had a successful, self-affirming experience since she learned to walk! She wrote: "I will be thirty-six years old in a few days and have lived most of those years hating God if there was one. What a miserable life I've had. As a child, life was terribly unhappy because my father was a violent person who beat my mother and six brothers. As an adult, my life was still one of turmoil. Almost two years ago, I attempted suicide and failed. After failing at the suicide attempt, I was on the verge of a nervous breakdown. I could see where I was headed. I wasn't able to eat. I lost nineteen pounds in three weeks. I wasn't able to sleep well, consequently I was awake early on Sundays when the 'Hour of Power' came on. At first I watched the program simply because there wasn't anything else to watch and I needed anything to keep my mind occupied and to hang on!

"Then, as the weeks passed I found myself deliberately turning on the program. Many Sundays I found myself, an unbeliever, drenched with tears as I discovered God's love and forgiveness.

"One evening when I was in a desperately low state, something literally brought me to my knees in my bedroom. Out of sheer desperation, and with a final realization that if I didn't get help I was going to die, I spoke to God. I didn't know how I was to speak to Him; I wasn't even convinced that He existed. My prayer was very short. It was the prayer of a thirty-six-year-old drowning woman who had nowhere else to turn. I simply told God I couldn't make it on my own. I needed help. The amazing thing is, He heard me and came to me. I know without a doubt that He was with me that night. Something happened!

"No dramatic changes took place overnight. I wasn't even aware at the time that the Lord had begun to work in me. But today, there have been such tremendous changes in my life that I can hardly believe that it is me! I stand in awe. Now I awaken in the morning and praise God for giving me breath for one more day rather than hurting because I lived one more day. I have grown to love Jesus more than words can express. I even care about myself!"

A peak experience at thirty-six! And she's got a peek—just a little glimpse—of what great things God has in store for her!

chapter nineteen

Strive and Arrive

YOU WANT PEAK EXPERIENCES? You need peak experiences! Without the peak experiences, no peek experiences, no vision of a hope-filled tomorrow. Peak experiences generate mental and emotional health in two obvious ways:

(1) They immediately boost our positive self-image, renew our sense of self-worth, and revitalize our self-esteem. That is a primary sign of a healthy personality.

(2) The peak experience, we have seen, produces a peek experience. Why is this so terribly significant? Because "Where there is no vision, the people perish," the Bible says. What, after all, is a "peek" experience? It's an encounter with HOPE! A surge of positive expectancy, an explosion of genuine optimism, an inner rush of possibility thinking about tomorrow, that's what the "peek" experience is. That all adds up to one word: HOPE! And without hope there is discouragement first, and without correction it will intensify, becoming depression, which, unheeded, can and will soon deepen to dark despair. And the will to live gives way to the will to die! So the Peak to Peek Principle touches the very taproot of human life!

In what way can I sum up all that I've said in this book?

Choose to succeed. Strive to arrive at a meaningful new goal. Successful persons survive because they work at it—be it marriage, business, religion, self-improve-ment, education, physical fitness, or whatever. You must strive . . . to arrive.

I'll sum it up in these six letters: S-T-R-I-V-E.

S—Start small.

T—Think possibilities.

R—Reach a little beyond your grasp.

I—Invest all you have in the dream.

V—Visualize victory.

E—Expect success.

As you will notice, the above sentences start with letters that spell out S-T-R-I-V-E.

Start small. Start today to reach out toward a new peak. "Your biggest problem, Dr. Schuller, will be inertia," Walt Frederick, a member of our church, was lecturing to me ten years ago. I was forty pounds overweight. Totally nonathletic. "I'm going to get you started—on a walking, then jogging, then running program," he announced. A week later, he met me at my office and escorted me on a one-mile hike—and we jogged the last sixty feet! We started small. One week later, he was back. We walked the same path—this time we jogged sixty to one hundred feet in the course of the mile. Week after week, we increased the jogging length. When I ran a whole city block, I accomplished an impossibility! It was a peak experience! Which gave rise to a new peek, at a higher peak! I tried for two blocks! Then six! Then ten! Then one mile! Then two miles! Then three miles, until I was running eight miles a morning! "Inch by inch anything's a cinch—yard by yard anything is hard." Start—and start small. Now, ten years later, and many pounds lighter, I'm in better shape than I've ever been in my whole life!

One out of every 435 persons in the U.S.A. today is a

millionaire. Almost all started small: a paycheck, some little money saved. The little was invested in a small house, or a little business, or a few stocks, or a couple of apartments to rent. Soon the little doubled: five thousand dollars doubled to ten thousand, ten thousand to twenty thousand. Soon it added up to a hundred thousand. That made the down payment on an investment worth five hundred thousand. It was sold for eight hundred thousand dollars and within ten or twenty years, a new millionaire was born! It's happening right now as you read this book! *The Peak to Peek Principle is working.*

While I was starting our church, in 1955, two men, Rich DeVos and Jay Van Andel, were starting a new sales organization with a clever marketing program in Ada, Michigan. (You can go anywhere from where you are!) All they had was a desk—and an idea! Today their business—Amway Corporation—has created dozens of millionaires out of policemen, teachers, and janitors! And Rich and Jay are reportedly worth many millions each! More important, they're using their success to build people, families, and stronger communities and churches, and doing more to relieve unemployment than anyone else I know!

George Johnson—a young black boy in Chicago—started selling products from barbershop to barbershop. Then he hit on an idea: hair straightener for blacks. He found a chemist—came up with a mixture—called it Afro-Sheen! Today his personal fortune is estimated in the tens of millions of dollars. How did he do it without powerful connections? (1) He Started small! (2) Thought possibilities! (3) Reached a little beyond his grasp! (4) Invested all he had: pride, purpose, power, dollars! (5) He Visualized success (this kept him going through dark times). (6) He Expected to Experience Expansions with responsible growth, and he did. Today he's a member of the church board of directors and a witness to the power of the Peak to Peek Principle.

Consider another member of our church board of directors: John Crean. With $250 he purchased some wood and rope and started making blinds for house trailers. He sold them to manufacturers of mobile homes, poured the money back into more wood and rope and made more: sold more, working out of his garage, until in a year the $250 grew to $10,000! A peak was reached. And he caught a peek at a new peak! (He'd take the $10,000 and build and sell his own mobile home!) He did. He succeeded! The Peak to Peek Principle was at work. Soon he was leasing a larger place and "making a few mobile homes"! He manufactured. He sold. He started small. Thought possibilities. Reached farther. Invested all he had. Visualized finished products successfully made and delivered. Expected success. Experienced success. Expanded. And that's the story of the nation's number 1 mobile home manufacturer, Fleetwood Enterprises. And in spite of fuel shortages and drastic market reverses, the company is solid, and according to *Fortune* magazine, one of the best-run companies in the top 500 American industrial corporations! He's a living illustration of the power of the Peak to Peek Principle.

She's one of our nation's most respected psychologists. Her name: Dr. Judy Huntsinger. She was an average homemaker. A wife. A mother. Her husband started working for me. He shared the dynamic philosophy and powerful psychology and creative theology contained in the words "possibility thinking." She looked over his shoulder as he listened to what we were teaching. "If it were true—if I could do and be anything I'd like to—then I'd love to be a psychologist and help the children in our public schools," she thought as she listened to the Peak to Peek Principle and started dreaming.

Result? (1) She Started. She went back to school. Of course, it took nerve. Remember the early lines of this book?

"It takes guts to leave the ruts."

She started. She started small; thought possibilities. Reached a little beyond her known or imagined ability (and discovered she had more inside her than she had ever realized). Experienced a "peak"—passed a year:

Got a new "peek"—and went on. Hit a new peak! Got a new "peek!" So she kept going. Invested her money and energies. Visualized a meaningful life at the end of the struggle. Expected somehow, someway, sometime to succeed. And she did! She has earned her Ph.D. in psychology and has demonstrated the power of the Peak to Peek Principle!

I know many people—several friends of mine—far more than millionaires in personal financial net worth, who have used this Peak to Peek Principle, and by following the S-T-R-I-V-E steps, they made it from almost nothing to financial security and independence. A friend who wants to remain unnamed used real estate as his vehicle. He earned a little and saved a little. He purchased a house with 20 percent down. He struggled to save $10,000 to buy a $50,000 home, borrowing $40,000. The house increased in value more than inflation. In three years he sold his house for $65,000. And after paying the mortgage, he had $25,000 left. Which means he more than doubled his investment in three years. The $25,000 enabled him to make the down payment on a $125,000 duplex (two adjoining apartments). Interest on the $100,000 loan, taxes, and depreciation kept him from having to pay income taxes. He painted, improved the property, and in four years sold it for $220,000! With a profit and some additional cash, he made the down payment on a $1,000,000 apartment complex. He managed it well. Improved it. In two years he sold it for $1,300,000. Now his "equity" or "net worth" or "fortune" or "cash after sale" added up to $500,000. He now had the 25 percent down payment on a $2,000,000 national franchised motel. He bought it at a low price because the owners were "absentee landlords" and had allowed service to decline. Under the new, enthusiastic management, he showed—in four years—such a good profit that he was offered $3,000,000 for the property and business. He counteroffered, "Sorry, I'll sell for 4,000,000!" The would-be buyers offered 3,500,000—and he accepted, to find himself looking at a personal fortune of $2,000,000 with all debts paid—

save for capital-gains tax! Beautiful! And in another way he demonstrated the power of the Peak to Peek Principle! Can you imagine how this fortune will escalate in ten years? Twenty years? As he continues to invest wisely?

Where could you be in ten years? In fifteen years? Or twenty-five years? If you really try? Yes STRIVE! Start small. Think possibilities: Reach out—just a little beyond your presumed abilities. Invest all you are and have and hope to be in your goal. Visualize growth and success. Expect to Expand as you build your base strong and solid!

Can a student who drops out of high school with a D average be expected to succeed! Does a teacher reach a point where she has to give up believing in the potential of a student to succeed?

If we have a juvenile delinquent on the block, must we continue to believe that he can't be a great human being someday?

Jerry Ross is a friend of mine. He was born in Flint, Michigan, in the toughest neighborhood there. His young days were spent in gang fights, and he has the scars to remind him of them. A juvenile delinquent, he dropped out of high school. He spent his days on the street. The only white kid on his block. He married at eighteen. Now, with a pregnant wife, he needed a job desperately.

At the same time, marriage problems were already on the way, and he was referred to a black marriage counselor, who tested him and said, "You should either be (a) a salesman or (b) a mechanic." He went to the General Motors school for mechanics, and with the grease in his nails and on his fingers he decided: "That's an awful way to earn a living." And walking by the used-car lot, he stopped to check out a used car and was soon noticed by the salesman. Within a week he decided to try his hand at selling used cars and did amazingly well. He was guaranteed a weekly salary of forty dollars. He was so enthused that he could "do something with my brain and not with my back!" One day a customer came in to look at his seventy-five dollar used cars. He was a furniture dealer who was advertising the sale of entire rooms of furniture with the promise that he would throw in a free car with every new room of furniture purchased. The cars that he threw in, of course, were the seventy-five dollar used cars that he would buy from Jerry Ross, the teenage used-car salesman.

"He liked me," Jerry Ross tells you, "and he said, 'Why don't you come to work for me?' It's more fun selling furniture than cars." Within two weeks, Jerry Ross became the top salesman—out of five or six—in the furniture shop and was earning $125 a week. The next week, he earned $175. To motivate him, the owner of the furniture shop promised him bonuses. At the end of the first year, he had earned twenty-eight thousand dollars. In 1959, that was a lot of money. And he was only nineteen years old. In the second year, he was made the manager of the three furniture stores that his boss owned. At the age of twenty he was put in charge of buying furniture from the manufacturers and distributors, hiring salesmen, and placing ads in the newspapers. In his second year, he made forty-two thousand dollars, mostly on bonuses from sales projections that were placed ridiculously high by the owner, who thought Jerry would never make it. But he succeeded in making the ridiculous projections by going back to the street and hiring his old buddies: dropouts from the street gang. One was a plumber, another a gas-station worker. A few were unemployed. They were black and white, of various nationalities and religions.

"To show you the kind of friends I had and grew up with," Jerry told me, "eleven of those guys are dead today. Five were murdered. Four are serving life sentences." After four years the store owner promised Jerry a preposterously high bonus if he could make an unrealistic sales figure. Everyone, including Jerry, was surprised when he made it. The owner refused to pay the bonus, however, and Jerry quit.

Three weeks later, at the age of twenty-four, he borrowed ten thousand dollars from his dad (who mortgaged his cottage to get the money for his son) and rented an empty six-thousand-square-foot store. He painted the building, fixed it up, then went to the furniture wholesalers, who knew him well. They agreed to fill his empty store with their merchandise if Jerry promised to sell enough carpet and pieces of furniture for cash in thirty days to pay for his inventory! In the first month of operation, he sold $200,000 worth, $100,000 in carpet alone. His net after cost was $50,000 for his first month! At the end of his first year, he had gross sales of $3,000,000, with a net profit of $500,000! Within the next eighteen months he opened twenty more stores throughout Michigan: "Worldwide Home Furnishings, Inc."

How did he do it? He simply used the Peak to Peek Principle! He approached investors and said, "I want to open a new store in Kalamazoo, Michigan (or wherever). I'll guarantee that it'll make $100,000 a year. It'll take me $51,000 to open it. I'll sell you 49 percent of the first year's profits for a $25,000 initial investment. In every case, the investors got more than $50,000 back at the end of the year for the $25,000 they invested in it," Jerry proudly reported.

By 1968, at the age of twenty-eight, Jerry Ross had built up a personal fortune of $7,000,000, which he invested in buildings which he then leased to corporations. At the age of thirty-eight he retired with $2,000,000 cash in the bank and $12,000,000 in solid real-estate investments.

Are there hopeless persons? There are no hopeless cases! Today Jerry is the proud father of nine children and has three grandchildren. As this book goes to press, he is only forty years of age and highly devoted to his Roman Catholic church and to his children and grandchildren.

"When I was young," Jerry says, "I asked a very wealthy man that I met in the furniture store, 'How do you get rich?' And he said to me, 'Jerry, get involved! Then things start happening.' This man explained, 'I bought lots of gas stations in town on the corners. The gas stations did very badly but I found myself owning corners of real estate. And the real estate turned out to be very profitable. The secret is to get involved.' Build a base. Make it solid. Keep expanding!" Of course: it's the power of the Peak to Peek Principle.

chapter twenty

How Possibility Thinkers Manage to Succeed

THE KEY WORD IS MANAGEMENT. Failure is never the
result of a lack of money, time, energy, opportunity,
talent, training, or connections. Failure is never the
result of problems, risks, frustrations, or difficult people. Likewise, the superachiever, the top-of-the-ladder
successful person isn't where he is because of what he
has or had; rather, because of what he *is*. He is a skilled
manager.

Some corporate giants with an empire that took time
to build have watched their wealth shrivel before their
eyes for lack of right management skills. They see a
Johnny-come-lately overtake and then pass them in the
marketplace. A rich youngster may lose his inherited
wealth through poor management, while a poor kid
from a deprived background, uneducated and oppressed,
breaks loose and makes his first million and goes on to
greater success.

The point is that it is not what you have but what you
are.

Are *you* a skillful manager? Management means the
control of resources so as to maximize the achievement
of predetermined objectives.

Let's test your management skills. To succeed, you
will have to develop your untapped potential as a manager in many areas.

I lecture at universities, conferences, seminars, and I

132

find that most management experts touch only on isolated areas: money, people, time. Let me review and reveal to your thoughtful mind the full field to which management skills must be applied. For to succeed as a manager in money management and fail in the management of the emotional life will probably turn a person into a multimillionaire alcoholic, drug addict, or eventual suicide.

Get ready now to become a "take-charge person" and build a reputation as a wise manager in these all-important areas:

Ideas

Possibility thinkers succeed because they learn to manage ideas. They form them carefully in their minds. They rationalize, intellectualize, conceptualize the ideas until they're sure that they are dealing with *ideas*, not *mere feelings*. Not infrequently they discover that they're dealing with feelings that can, in fact, reveal or give birth to authentic ideas or previously nondiagnosed, nonarticulated principles.

(A) Form them.

Often I've had enthusiastic people call me in an almost hysterical state: "I have to talk to you; I've got this possibility idea!"

My answer is always the same: "Write me a letter and put it on one page."

That, of course, forces them to give written form to their dream, desire, concern, or possibility.

(B) Firm them.

Good management means avoiding waste. To manage ideas, you must avoid wasting the idea—throwing it away simply because it's impossible. Hence firming is always the first step for every good idea. You never abort a good idea. You give it a chance to be born. Before you waste time, money, energy on that idea, you firm it up: test it out to determine whether or not it deserves your commitment. The firming stage of idea management is the question-asking phase. You simply test the success potential by asking the right questions. More on this when we get to decision management. If the idea passes the test, you then firm it up with a commitment. You will not let the idea get away. A great idea is a terrible thing to let die.

(C) Farm them.

You have formed the idea and you have firmed the idea. . . . Now farm the idea. You plant the idea. You invest seed thoughts without assurance that there will be no crop failure. You plant the seed, take a chance, weed it, feed it, and cultivate it.

There are two classes of farmers in the world: the landowners and the land renters. You may farm your idea by leasing it to someone who has the interest, time, capital, and ability to develop its potential. You take a "rental" from the tenant farmer in the form of a royalty, franchise, or license fee or a percentage of the profit.

You may "farm" your idea by selling it outright. Or you may choose to "work your own land": control your own idea by developing it yourself.

Whatever you do, you preserve the profit potential in the idea by protecting it from landing in the scrap pile of great ideas. Only you can make the decision to discard this possibility-pregnant idea. You won't make the mistake of discarding old things as trash when they have achieved value as antiques. You'll farm that idea through heat and cold, dry spells and floods, summer and winter . . . until you harvest the fruit or your idea-managing efforts. You have formed, firmed, and farmed. Now you can . . .

(D) Frame your ideas.

Yes, you win your award. You hang it proudly on the wall. You display your badge of achievement without shame. You do not treat this lightly, as if it were a trivial document sent to join that pile of papers collecting dust. You frame it, to preserve it and to inspire you with visions of greater challenges waiting to become greater achievements. You'll harness the Peak to Peek Principle as you manage ideas masterfully.

Money

It's very interesting to note that great idea managers seldom have long-lasting money problems. They have learned this terribly important lesson: no person, no institution, no country, no business has a money problem. It's always an idea problem. So tiny Singapore leads the free nations in generating, creating wealth with the smallest inflation rate (3.6 percent) during a period of wild inflation. They simply harvested some better ideas in that period of history than the United States. The richest country saw its dollar plunge. Money management gets down to idea management. Money flows to dynamic, positive ideas.

How do you get the ideas to manage money successfully? For one thing, discover and absorb the basic topic of this book: the Peak to Peek Principle.

Opportunities

So possibility thinkers succeed because they manage ideas wisely; they never let money problems stop them cold. And so they go on to manage opportunities productively. They see opportunities where and when others do not. How? They are tuned to look for a need, knowing that every need is an opportunity waiting to be seized. They see, then seize opportunities. Even if they're too busy, or overloaded, or financially committed, they do not allow the opportunity to escape. They seize it by laying seige to it. They surround it to attack and control it later. They take an option on it and buy time to solve the problems that may keep them from capitalizing on the opportunity at the moment.

What if the opportunity won't wait? They then exercise a companion management skill: time management.

Time

Possibility thinkers succeed also because they are good time managers. The secret: 1. Analyze. 2. Prioritize. 3. Amortize. 4. Organize. 5. Supervise.

1. *Analyze* your time expenditures. Is this time expenditure necessary: (I refuse to do anything if I can hire someone else to do it.) Is there a faster way to do what I'm doing and get the job done as well or better? (I never take a trip if a telephone call can get the job done.) Can this wait? How long? How will the delay affect the cost?

2. *Prioritize* your time expenditures. Reevaluate your time. It should be worth more the more experienced you are. You get better ideas. You face brighter opportunities. What was important yesterday might have to be discarded from your schedule today. Be brave. It takes guts to leave the ruts. Every person, every business, every institution needs to constantly review and reevaluate its priorities.

How? Ask the basic questions: (a) What do I want to accomplish? (b) If I keep going the way I'm going, will I succeed? (c) If I succeed, will I really be pleased and proud of myself?

3. *Amortize* your time after you have realigned your priorities. For instance: The top priority in my life for thirty years has been a successful marriage. So I amortize my time accordingly. Every Monday night is blocked out on my calendar as a date-with-my-wife night. No wonder our marriage is super. And keeps getting amazingly richer. Why? We're watching the Peak to Peek Principle at work. As you amortize your time, you ask yourself: Will this advance me closer to my objective?

One of my personal goals is physical fitness. So I calendar time to run. Another objective is spiritual aliveness, so I calendar a weekly inspirational experience in the church of my choice. One of my objectives is to "keep up always" and never burn out. So I amortize time regularly for rest, retreat, and renewal. Amortizing time is really easy if you've done your homework (prioritized your values).

4. *Organize*. Plan your time and stick with your plan. You've learned the secrets of successful time management. The result: You'll get more important things accomplished. You'll reach a new peak of accomplishment and get a new peek into life's real possibilities. You'll be tapping into the Peak to Peek Principle.

Surprise! You'll find that as you learn to manage time better, you'll get along with people better.

5. *Supervise*. Now supervise your time expenditures. Never surrender leadership. Maintain control. Allow no one or no thing to spoil your plan. How? Simple. Prepare an annual calendar. Write in the dates on which you have time committed to achieve your objectives. When someone, or something, comes along to detour you, use your priorities to determine whether you should be responsive or graciously frigid to the uninvited intrusion and unwelcome interruption.

"I'm sorry, I'm committed on that night," or "sorry, but my calendar is full." It's so simple. Management, remember, is another word for control.

A friend of mine has learned that she needs two evenings a month alone to think and catch up on projects. During the month, her well-filled calendar has two nights with the word COMMITMENT scrawled in. When unanticipated invitations (more often than not, tempting) arise, she is neither pressured nor intimidated into saying yes. She answers, "Let me check my calendar. Oh, I'm sorry (she almost always is sincerely sorry), but I have a commitment that night."

People

Possibility thinkers succeed because they learn how to manage people who help them reach their objectives. Idea problems? They find creative people who can help generate successful ideas. That's why I've hired consultants and still do.

Money problems? Hire an expert who can come up with bright money-management ideas.

Time problems? Someone somewhere can release me from many time-consuming, nonproductive activities. Someone else can help me organize my time. Someone else will provide what I really need: a relationship that I can reward by sharing the fruits of my success. So I won't be lonely when I've got it made.

You can see that people management is as important if not more so than time or money management. We've all known people who have made money but failed dismally in their personal relationships.

How *do you* manage people successfully? There are four words that are timeless guideposts: (1) Be friendly. (2) Be fair. (3) Be frank. (4) Be firm.

We see that skillful managers know how to manage people who, in turn, help them manage their inherited and acquired talents.

Talent and Training

So superachievers have outstanding talent. Not necessarily so. But possibility thinkers have learned how to manage wisely and productively the talents and training they have acquired. The shores of the world are littered with wasted and mismanaged talents.

What is the ultimate talent? It's dedication, determination, drive, ambition. "The real talent is the drive to win," a baseball coach said to me.

I watched a young girl named Carol Schuller stand at home plate. Two years before, she was almost killed. Now she wears a uniform of a softball league.

"How do you expect to play ball when you can't run?" I asked her.

She faced me with flashing eyes. "People who hit home runs don't have to run."

As I write this chapter, I've watched her get three hits—getting herself to first base. "If I want a single, all I have to do is hit a triple," she declared.

Watching her standing at bat is like beholding a little volcano of pent-up energy waiting to erupt. She's my daughter. Her talent? It's her drive to arrive.

How good a manager of your own talent and training are you? Can you accept advice? Take constructive criticism? Are you willing to be trained, retrained, restrained? Are you open to big-thinking ideas? Are you receptive to enthusiastic, motivational forces and faces?

Here's the real secret of managing your talent. Choose to be success oriented—not ego involved.

"I don't want my own way. I just want to succeed," I said as I publicly changed direction in a project. I added, "I'd rather be right and succeed than be wrong and have my own way."

Energy

Skillful managers of talent see their success generating enthusiasm. And this enthusiasm generates fantastic energy. Dynamic achievers seem to have a constant supply of high energy.

Are the top-of-the-ladder people more energetic? Are the losers cursed with an inherited inclination to fatigue? Do the winners know how to manage their energy? Of course. They avoid wasting energy. (Remember: Management means control. Control means avoiding waste.) How?

(1) By avoiding negative thinking. Nothing produces fatigue like discouragement, frustration, jealousy, fear, anxiety, inferiority feelings, or thoughts of failure.

(2) By avoiding negative programming. I carefully select the books I read, programs I listen to, persons I allow to come into my close circle of affection.

(3) Drawing close to energy-stimulating persons and projects. There are positive people, who make you feel great when you're around them. They fill your mind with positive ideas. Giant possibilities begin to unfold in the mental climate generated in their company.

If you can manage ideas, talent, time, opportunities, money, people, you should now learn to manage your energy. Eat right, sleep right, think right, exercise right, pray right, read right, fellowship right. You'll be amazed at the energy that seems endless.

You'll have enough energy to try to scale that mountain peak. You'll make it, and from that vantage point, with a peek into the undiscovered possibilities beyond, you'll be using that powerful Peak to Peek Principle.

Risk Management

You can see now how possibility thinkers accomplish the impossible. If you have ideas, opportunities, money, time, people, talent and training, energy, what more do you need?

You need the skill to manage risk-taking ventures. There's no success without risk-management skills. Essentially the secret is to know that, without risk, death is certain. Unless farmers are willing to risk losing their seed, they won't be able to grow food. The human race would then face mass starvation.

One of the most demonic of all contemporary negative thoughts loose in our society is the "let's eliminate risks" mentality.

Possibility thinkers soon learn this lesson. There's something wrong with the best idea. No project is without potential fault or risk.

Here's a basic lesson in theology. When God gets you where He wants you, you won't be able to do what you have to do without risk. Naturally; that's what the word "faith" means. When God lays His dream for your life into your thinking, it will be humanly impossible. That's His way of making sure you (1) have faith, (2) will seek His help, (3) can be trusted with the grand success He plans as a surprise at the top of the peak.

Nothing great happens until someone is willing to risk something: prestige or money.

Risk management, then, becomes a Siamese twin to a companion management skill called:

Decision Management

Risk takers are not fools. They become wise decision makers.

How?

(1) They list the alternatives.

(2) They summarize their options.

(3) They clarify their values to eliminate contradictions. (Risk-taking decision making is easy if your value system is not confused and the alternatives can be weighed and options considered.)

(4) They carefully separate decisions from problems. Decision managers never bring the problem-solving phase into the decision-making phase, or they have surrendered the leadership of the positive possibilities to the impossible problem.

Problem Management

Every significant project I ever undertook, including the construction of the Crystal Cathedral, was impossible when we made the decision to proceed. Why did we go ahead, then? Because the idea had so much integrity that to refuse to try simply because it appeared impossible would have been immoral. And in every case when we made the right decision we found amazing solutions to what so many were sure were unsolvable problems. Make a mountain-tackling decision (a peak decision) and you'll be astounded at the creative ideas and inventive visions (peeks) that will unfold.

Therefore decision-management skills must be matched by problem-management skills.

Is there a secret in reaching the bottom line that enables some persons to be successful problem managers? Of course. It's maintaining a positive mental outlook. Every problem is viewed as a challenge—not as a threat. There is nothing wrong with a problem unless it prevents you from thinking constructively. To an impossibility thinker, every problem holds unseen dangers. To a possibility thinker, every problem is a growth experience.

For a million years or more, the rock stood silently overlooking Malibu Beach, in southern California. In recent years, a new homeowner looked up at it above his house and decided it presented a potential threat to his safety. Organizing his neighbors, he launched a class-action suit against the state of California to have the rock removed. The state decided it would remove the rock. Bulldozers attacked it to no avail. It was wedged deeply into the mountainside, like an impacted wisdom tooth.

Brett Livingston Strong, a twenty-three-year-old visiting Australian, watched the progress—or lack thereof. He saw in the rock not a threat but an opportunity. After days of struggling, using helicopters and bulldozers, the rock came tumbling down and landed in the middle of the highway fronting the Pacific coast. First on the scene was the young Australian. "I'll buy it," he said. "For one hundred dollars," he said to an unbelieving highway official, who gladly accepted his offer. "It's yours," he replied; "you have two days to get it off the road."

Now the young foreigner, without money or contacts, owned a twenty-ton rock. (Talk about possibility thinking.) A problem? No way. He saw only a possibility. He proceeded to raise twenty thousand dollars from the merchants in the Century City shopping area, convincing them that a display of the rock would be good for their business. In raising the capital, he had scaled his first peak and solved his first problem—and caught a peek at a new possibility. He covered the rock with canvas, bought a jackhammer, and started secretly sculpting the face of a famous man who lay dying in a hospital a few miles away. When John Wayne, the celebrated movie star, who was dying of cancer, heard about it, he left his bed to see what was happening.

"I like it," he said, "but why me? Why the face of John Wayne?"

"Because, sir," Brett answered, "the rock reminds me of you—tough to bring down."

Today that rock has been sold for one million dollars.

What is the lesson here? It is that what one person sees as a threat, another views as an opportunity.

"But," you might say, "that rock really might have fallen on the houses below and perhaps killed someone."

No way. They now know it was so deeply embedded that it couldn't have fallen in a million years.

As a matter of fact, the removal of the rock caused mud slides that did damage to some of the houses of those who wanted it gone. The rock was nature's retaining wall.

Ask yourself how successful a manager you are. If you can manage ideas, opportunities, money, time, people, energy, talent, risks, decisions, and problems, you've got it made. Right? Not quite. Not unless you have learned how to manage yourself.

Managing yourself encompasses learning how to manage your failures. After all, you may miss every once in a while. No pitcher ever struck out the first twenty-seven men to come to bat. No batter ever averaged one thousand in a season. No quarterback ever completed all his passes.

You manage your misses by learning from every failure. A failure that teaches you something has real value.

You learn also how to manage your successes. You must let each success solidify and expand your power base. You must manage your imagination. With each new peak scaled, you channel your imagination to envision new fields to conquer. You harness the Peak to Peek Principle.

Never allow yourself to lose control; that is, the management of your imagination. For what you see is what you'll be. If you surrender the leadership of your imagination to fear, thoughts of failure, or frustration, you'll start to fall backward. Keep your imagination focused on new peaks to climb and you'll keep moving forward.

chapter twenty-one

Never Believe in Never

I RECALL AN INVITATION that came one September to visit the Honorable Hubert Humphrey in his Minnesota apartment. We had been friends for years. It was my honor to have him listen regularly to my national television program, "Hour of Power." He could catch the program in Washington and in Minnesota.

My plane would soon land in Minneapolis. What would I say to the Senator? I had just been told by a family spokesman that the cancer he had fought so bravely for so many years had spread beyond reasonable hope for containment.

I was welcomed by a close family friend. "We'll go straight to the apartment. The Senator and his wife, Muriel, are anxious to see you," he said. His voice was soft, slow, low—exposing his grave concern.

"What can I do for him?" I asked.

"For the first time since he got news of his cancer, many years ago, the Senator seems to be resigned to stay home and die," the family friend answered. And now, as he waited for a red light to change, he turned his head and with desperation in his eyes and voice he continued, "We thought, Dr. Schuller, perhaps you could inspire him to go back to Washington. Even if he only lives another three months—as the doctor indicated —we believe these weeks could be so much more mean-

145

ingful to him in the Washington environment than if he
simply stayed here and waited for death to call him."

I prayed silently for guidance. "What shall I say to
the Senator?" I prayed!

"NEVER BELIEVE IN NEVER"

Hubert Horatio Humphrey was dressed for my arrival.
He was very lean. It had been some months since I had
last seen him. "If he doesn't want to face Washington
and his friends looking so weak, should I even try to
inspire him to return for his last twelve weeks of life?" I
prayed to God with this question. Deep in my soul I
heard God's answer: "Yes! I have great plans for him
yet!" "How can I, Lord, motivate him to make this
decision?" Immediately I was given guidance and I
heard myself ask him, "What were some of the most
inspiring sentences, slogans, and sayings that have inspired you in your life?" "Well, one that has meant so
much to Muriel and me these last months is your
ministry's slogan, Bob, 'God loves you and so do I.' And
in view of my condition, Muriel and I would like to
make that sentence our Christmas Card. May we?"
"Of course!" I answered. They did. It humbled—but
pleased—me. "Go on," I urged, "what are some others?"
Again simply because I was there, he remembered
and quoted my Possibility Thinkers' Creed—years before, he'd requested a copy—when he first contracted
cancer. I recited it; he joined in, knowing it from
memory.

THE POSSIBILITY THINKER'S CREED

When faced with a mountain, *I will not quit*. I will
keep on striving until I climb over, find a path through,
tunnel underneath, or simply stay and turn the mountain into a gold mine with God's help.

"Share others with me," I urged. "Bring me my black notebook, Muriel?" he asked, and told her where she could find it. She returned and handed him a thick, well-worn notebook. His eyes were sparkling again! I saw energy returning! As he "recalled" and "reread" the old inspirational passages, his spirit renewed! After a half hour I burst out with the gusto we often mutually demonstrated; "Hubert! When are you going back to Washington? You know that everybody in that town will really pay attention to you now." Our eyes, hearts, and spirits electrically connected! I knew I was divinely guided. He brightened, sat straighter, turned to his beautiful wife and said, "Yes, Muriel. I've got to get back there!" We prayed. We embraced. He insisted on walking out of the apartment, seeing me down the elevator—to my waiting car; and I last saw him alive with his arm around Muriel under the setting autumn sun of a clear Minnesota sky. His hand reached high as he waved good-bye. And my car pulled out—back to the airport. "You'll probably never see him again," the family friend said. And my heart was crying out, *"Never* believe in never!" I boarded my plane. The next day, I heard it on the news. "President Jimmy Carter will leave California today, where he has been speaking. He announced that Air Force One would make a stop in Minnesota to pick up Senator Hubert H. Humphrey, who has decided to make a last return to Washington, D.C." And I cried a little!

The honors, plaudits, awards, tributes of all of Washington showered him in the next few weeks. He called me at the peak of public glory. "It's been really beautiful," he said as he caught a peek at the esteem with which even his old political enemies held him.

"It's ironic, Hubert," I said, "that while Richard Nixon defeated you and became the President, he is today in virtual exile at his San Clemente home, only twenty miles from where I'm sitting. Now you, the defeated, are the honored, while he, the victor, is being showered with dishonor and public scorn. Can he ever be forgiven? Should he ever be forgiven? And who could be the catalyst of such grace?" I threw out the questions. "I think he's suffered enough," Humphrey answered.

"Well, the only person who could offer the Psalm of pardon," I offered, "would be someone (1) who was on the opposite side of the political fence, (2) someone who commands the respect of all of America. And," I continued, "since offering a friendly, forgiving gesture would be so dangerous to the compassionate donor, it would have to be (3) someone who wouldn't have to worry about being reelected." His voice boomed, "Sounds like I'm the man." He laughed loudly, saying, "I don't worry about being reelected!"

I alerted Nixon's office in San Clemente. Two days later, the old rivals were talking on the phone. And less than a month later, Muriel invited Richard Nixon to sit with her as her deceased husband's casket rested under the Capitol Rotunda for the Washington funeral. I remembered how deep was the bitter feeling after the Nixon-Humphrey presidential campaign. "They'll never speak to each other again," I heard a confidant say.

"Never believe in never," I silently thought!

When Nixon left Washington after Watergate—in disgrace—everyone agreed, "He'll never be able to show his face in this town again." Never believe in never!

After a quarter of a century as a pastor in one church, in one place, I've learned that God lives in a realm called forever. And there is no never in forever!

As this book is being printed, we are putting the finishing touches on the Crystal Cathedral. "He'll never make it," my critics said.

Today I see how it did happen.

October 1975—We borrow $200,000 from the bank to retain architect Philip Johnson. "I don't want any ceiling to come between my eyes—my spirit—and the sky," I declared. "Make it all glass."

November 1975—We unveil the architect's plan: a six-inch plastic model of a four-pointed star-shaped, all-glass Cathedral—414 feet long from point to point! We accept the plans. And order him to proceed.

December 1975—He reports a cost estimate: $7,000,000. I almost faint. Desperate! I read my own books! Start small. Think possibilities. Reach beyond your known abilities. Invest all you have in it. Expect to experience success! And *never believe in never*.

January 1976—Architect reports, "The structure is viable from an engineering point of view. The City Building Department okays our preliminary request to build it."

February 1976—I'm overwhelmed. How can we pay off the $200,000 bank loan? Where could we ever get $7,000,000?

April 1976—I call on a wealthy man. I show him the plans. "It'll never happen unless we get a big lead-off gift—like one million dollars?" "I'd like to but can't." He's blunt.

I prayed, "O God, I'm so thankful he wants to give a million—is it possible for you to figure out a way for him to do what he'd like to do but can't?"

The next day is Good Friday. 11:06 A.M. He calls me. "Dr. Schuller, it's not a question of if—only of how and when." That was his way of telling me that he would in fact give $1,000,000!

May 1976—The anonymous donor delivers 55,000 shares of stock at $18⅛ a share—good for $1,000,000!

June 1976—We decide to build a full basement (one acre!) to accommodate the choirs, music department, orchestra and concert requirements. The cost goes up from $7,000,00 to $10,000,000.

June 1976—I fly to Chicago. I ask W. Clement Stone to give $1,000,000. It's a lovely dinner in his mansion. But his answer is negative. We pause at the doorway in the moonlight before my driver is to return me to the airport hotel. We pray. The next morning, my phone rings. It's Clem Stone. "Schuller, tell you what I'll do:

If you can collect the other $9,000,000 *in cash,* I'll give the tenth million!" I'm ecstatic!

The Peak to Peek Principle is working!

"Never believe in never," I tell myself.

September 1976—We launch the sale of memorial windows (there are 10,000 in the Cathedral) at $500 each.

January 1977—All 10,000 are sold! With $1,000,000 cash on hand (the balance to come in over twenty-four months), I'm overjoyed. The project looks great!

February 1977—Bad news. I read a report that a new California environmental law will prohibit construction of any buildings if more than 50 percent of the exterior walls are glass! Our project is doomed! It's 100 percent glass! *"Never believe in never!"*

I call the mayor of the city—and the head of the Building Department. "That's right, Reverend, that's the new law—for all building permits issued after this month," I am told.

Desperate, I call the architect, and just hours before the month's end, we turned the architect's first drawings in to City Hall. The project is approved! Only a few days before the new regulation goes into effect!

March 1977—I'm high. I receive reports that the money from monthly payments of windows is coming in! We should have another million by summer!

June 1977—I'm in Hawaii on the way to Australia. I'm concerned about the cost of the project. I call Philip Johnson's partner, John Burgee. "John, can you assure me that the building can still be built for $10,000,000?" He's silent. Then he begins, "Yes, Dr. Schuller; however, inflation is taking its toll—and you may have to leave the basement unfinished." It hurts, but I'm relieved. "Then, finish the drawings and send them down to our builder, Clair Peck, and we'll let out the bids," I direct. "When I get back, in August, from Australia, let's hope we have a firm bid—and can start building.

August 1977—I'm called to an urgent meeting. "The bids are in." The contractor, myself, the architect (John Burgee), and Victor Andrews (a close friend and adviser) meet, and I get the horrible news.

"The bids total a little more than $10,000,000," the contractor's representative starts breaking the news to me as gently as he can, continuing, "actually they total $13,400,000." I feel weak in my knees. Vic Andrews asks the obvious question: "Does that include everything?"

"Well, you'll have to put a 10 percent contingency fee on top of that," the contractor offers, explaining, "a normal project always runs into unforeseen building expenses that average 10 percent more than the contracts add up to." That immediately brings the price to over $14,700,000! I see the project becoming impossible! Only eight weeks before, I'd had the assurance from John Burgee that we could build it for $10,000,000 by "not finishing off the basement." I don't know what to do. I ask to be excused. My eyes fill with tears. I feel that I will have to abandon the project and let down everybody who had contributed (about $3,000,000) toward it already. I come back to the meeting room. I simply announce: "Gentlemen, if that's all, you're excused and we'll have to review the project to see if it's still viable." They go their ways. I prepare a news release announcing "The Crystal Cathedral project will be abandoned," explaining: "When the bids came in, the project went from $10,000,000 to nearly $15,000,000, which exceeds our capabilities." A vast weight seems to flow from my shoulders at the prospect of abandoning the project that is beyond our abilities at this point. I go to the man who gave me the first $1,000,000. I tell him about the problem. He says, "Schuller, dig a hole for the foundation. Somehow, someway, the money will come." It was encouraging. Back in my office, I find a letter from a Roman Catholic Sister in an eastern city telling me, "Congratulations on the Crystal Cathedral! We wanted to build a new wing on the hospital and everyone said it was impossible with the inflating costs. But I said, 'If Schuller can find money to build a Crystal Cathedral, don't you suppose we could find the money to build a new hospital?' That turned the decision-making meeting around, and I'm proud to tell you that we are going to build a new hospital. Thanks to the inspiration of your Crystal Cathedral project!"

Then and there, I know we cannot abandon the project. For we would inspire many projects to expire if we retired!

We go back to the contractor and ask him, "Can you build just the shell of the structure, and if so, what would that cost?" He replies, "I can build that for $9,200,000." "Then, that's what we will build," I declare. After all, we have about $2,000,000 in the bank. Blueprints are almost paid for. So we announce the ground-breaking ceremony!

December 4, 1977—Ground-breaking is held! Thousands of people gather. National television cameras are whirring. News appears in newspapers and magazines across the country. The Crystal Cathedral is under construction, in Garden Grove, California! But the terrible truth is that I know all we have is $2,000,000 in hand, the biggest bank commitment that we can find from anyone is from Farmers and Merchants Bank, in Garden Grove, promising the maximum of their legal loan capability, which is $4,000,000. That is still $3,000,000 short of covering the cost of the shell. But we convince the contractor, Mr. Peck, that we ought to collect that $3,000,000 from window money that will come in during the year and a half of anticipated construction time. Now the pictures of the cathedral begin to appear across America. In *Time*. In *Newsweek*. In *Vogue*. In *Architectural Review*. And now on "60 Minutes," with Dan Rather. And on Phil Donahue's talk show. And on the "Mike Douglas Show." On the NBC "Today" program. I am asked for interviews from major press people from Ireland, England, Australia, and South America! Suddenly the project becomes celebrated. And with that, the criticism mounts.

March 1978—An urgent meeting is called by the
contractor. His Legal Department advises him that he
cannot continue to sign the contracts and proceed with
the construction on the "hope and faith that the extra
$3,000,000 is going to come in in the next eighteen
months from unpredictable offerings." We are told,
"Either have a firm bank commitment for the other
$3,000,000 or come up with the other $3,000,000 cash,
or we close construction down."

"How soon do we need the extra $3,000,000?" I ask.
"We'll need $600,000 deposited in the bank in sixty
days. Another $1,000,000 by July. And another $1,400,000
by the middle of October of this year."

Never believe in never! I have to keep giving myself this positive encouragement. I write an urgent letter to all my friends across America. And in thirty days
the $600,000 cash is available. July will come soon.
Where would we get another $1,000,000 cash? We pray
and decide we'll try to make a single collection of
$1,000,000 on a single offering in our church! Impossi-
ble? That gave God a chance to work a miracle! I
discover that a small apartment that I purchased for
$36,000 on the ocean front eight years before with an
$8,000 inheritance from my father's estate has now
inflated in value until it has a market value of just under
$200,000! I arrange to get a new bank loan, drawing
$150,000 cash out of the equity, and tell the church
board that on the $1,000,000 Sunday, I'd make the
lead-off gift of $150,000. I hopefully expect them to
match me. "You'll never collect $1,000,000 on a single
Sunday!" many people predict. But never believe in
never!

Sunday, June 18, 1978—We have one of the largest
crowds in the history of our church. My daughter,
Carol, has sold her horse for $400 and drops 400 one-
dollar bills into the offering plate! Yes, hundreds of our
members do as well and better! The offerings total
$1,400,000! We made it. Construction can keep going!

September 1978—We'll need another $1,000,000 by the middle of October. Where will it come from? Out of the blue I receive a letter from Chicago, Illinois, from a person I've never met. "I've seen the picture of the Crystal Cathedral. It deserves to be built. Would a $1,000,000 gift from an elderly couple help you?" It is a clear miracle, to my mind! I fly to Chicago. I meet the gentleman. I promise I will maintain his anonymity. I hear him tell me that he will deliver the $1,000,000 gift by the middle of October.

October 1, 1978—A letter arrives! I open it. Inside is the check for $1,000,000!

November and December 1978—Another $1,000,000 comes in from window sales—and now we are offering stars to hang from the ceiling, for $500 each.

March 1979—I'm invited to the birthday party of the elderly gentleman in Chicago who gave me the $1,000,000. I deliver a gift to him at the small party. He slips an envelope to me. "I like to give gifts on my birthday," he says. I open it and out falls another $1,000,000 check to move the Crystal Cathedral beyond the shell stage toward the usable stage!

April 1979—The Organ Committee presents the report to me that the pipe organ that we planned to move out of our existing sanctuary into the Crystal Cathedral will be inadequate. It will cost nearly $1,000,000 to supply all the other parts, pipes, and console necessary to fill this huge Cathedral with adequate organ music! Virgil Fox, famed organist, telephones me and says: "Less than that would be terrible."

June 1979—A dear friend, Hazel Wright, Chicago, Illinois, invites me to her home. And offers $1,000,000 to cover the organ costs! Another miracle!

October, November, December 1979—More money comes in from the window sales and from the sales of stars.

December 31, 1979—We have collected $12,000,000 in cash, including the solid commitment of W. Clement Stone! With the addition of the organ and added inflationary expenses, the cost has now gone up to $16,000,000.

But we're only $4,000,000 short!

January 1980—"Nobody has a money problem—it's only an idea problem." I recall my own words in a lecture that I had given to top corporate executives at the University of California at Irvine. Now I pray that God will give us an idea to raise the last $4,000,000. I pray that we will be able to open the doors of the Crystal Cathedral on September 14, 1980, debt free! I pray that we might be able to give the entire offering from the first Sunday and onward to help great causes of hungry and hurting people around the world. If in fact we can open the Cathedral debt free, we will have created a huge place where we can attract great numbers of people, and motivate and inspire them to give generous offerings to sustain and support missionary projects around the world!

February 1980—We announce the plan to raise the last $4,000,000. We are going to try to sell each of the 3,000 seats for $1,500 each. That will bring us home free! Beverly Sills has agreed to perform a benefit concert on May 13 for the premier event in the Crystal Cathedral. We promise our friends that a memorial plaque with their names and their cities will be permanently affixed to the opera-style seats in the pews of the Crystal Cathedral. Can we succeed?

I make a trip to Vancouver, Canada. And my friends promise me that "Canada wants to buy an entire balcony of 300 seats for the Beverly Sills event! Count on us for $450,000!" This project is off to a good start. I come home and find a letter on my desk from Frank and Barbara Sinatra enclosing a check for $3,000 for two seats! The telephone rings. It's my friend Mickey Rooney calling from New York City. "My wife and I want to buy two seats."

Incredible? Yes! And no! Nothing is impossible with God! For God lives in forever land and there is no never in forever! *But I am writing this in February 1980, confident that the next peak is in view.*

May 13, 1980—The house is sold out! The famous, the super rich, and many ordinary beautiful people who have sacrificed greatly to collect a $1,500 offering fill the place. The Crystal Cathedral is enclosed. Beverly Sills fills the cathedral with glorious music! We have raised the last $4,000,000! Now we can spend June, July, and August planting the grass, cleaning the windows. And preparing for the grand dedication! On Sunday, September 7, I shall conduct the last service in the old church. I shall carry the pulpit Bible out at the close of the service and walk from the old church into the new, open doors of the Crystal Cathedral. The congregation shall follow me. And we shall prepare on Sunday, September 14, 1980, to celebrate the twenty-fifth anniversary of the organization of the ministry by dedicating the Crystal Cathedral debt free to the glory of God! And we shall take the entire offering to launch what will amount to a more than $1,000,000 emergency medical-relief center, serving over 300,000 Indians who live in incredibly medically deprived poverty pockets of the jungles of Mexico near the Guatemalan border.

The grandest dream has come true. A beautiful monument has turned into an instrument. An instrument that can generate more good for more people around the world than any of us ever imagined!

I remember what Alfred North Whitehead said: "Great dreams of great dreamers are never fulfilled, they are always transcended."

Our dreams have come true. Always!
Never believe in never!

What are your dreams? Pick a peak. Set a goal.
"I've tried losing weight so often and I'm just des-

tined to be fat. I'll never be thin." Never believe in never!

"I tried to quit smoking," or "I've tried to get off of drugs—I can never succeed." Never believe in never!

"I lost so much. I'll never regain my losses."
Never believe in never!

"We'll never be able to make our marriage work."
Never believe in never.

"I'll never graduate—or get the education I missed."
Never believe in never.

*   *   *

"I'll never walk again. My leg has been amputated."
Never believe in never.

"They crucified Jesus. They buried Him. We'll never hear from Him again."
Never believe in never.

chapter twenty-two

Pick a Peak

I HAVE HAD THE PRIVILEGE of becoming friends with a number of great people in this country and around the world. And I'm constantly amazed to find that the supersuccessful, top-of-the-ladder people are, in reality, very commonplace persons. I always thought great people were uniquely gifted or remarkably talented with some mythic, mystical, or charismatic quality that was most extraordinary and unique. But I am now convinced that such is seldom, if ever, the case. Great people are no different from you or me. They have simply made bigger decisions and set their minds on nobler goals. Great people are ordinary people who've committed themselves to extraordinary goals. They have seized a bigger opportunity, the opportunity that made them bigger persons. Larger goals released in their imaginations remarkable visions, peeks, glimpses into their future. Big people are really common people who dare to think bigger, dream bigger dreams. So greatness is the result of a commitment to unusually great dreams.

I challenge you to begin to believe that you have something beautiful and positive to give our world! Something great is stored up inside of you! The key to releasing the qualities, talents, and capacities you have is dynamic self-confidence. How do you get that?

Pick a peak! Find a goal.

Not long ago, I checked into a motel prior to a speaking engagement. It was late in the evening, and the lobby was empty except for the desk clerk. As I was unpacking, I reached for my toothbrush and realized that I had forgotten to pack my toothpaste. "Well, no problem," I thought to myself. "There's a dispensing machine down the hall." So I walked down the corridor and stood before the vending machine studying the contents. Behind the glass were all kinds of goodies: razor blades, pocketbooks, combs, and little tubes of toothpaste!

All I had to do was insert two quarters into the slot and my problem would be solved. I had no change, so I went to the desk and got four quarters. When I returned to the dispenser, I dropped in the first quarter . . . clink. Then I inserted the second quarter . . . clink. I pushed the red button below the tube of toothpaste and waited. Nothing happened! It didn't work! So I pressed the coin-return lever, and my quarters returned.

"Okay," I thought, "let's give it another Schuller try." I dropped the first quarter in . . . clink. Then the second quarter . . . clink. (I even used the other two quarters for good luck!) I pushed the button . . . again nothing happened!

Still no toothpaste! I paused for a moment, staring at all the things behind that glass—just out of my reach. "Think positive," I said aloud. So I pressed the button again. Nothing!

A little frustrated at this point, I pushed the coin-return lever, recovered my quarters, and went back to the front desk. I told the man my problem, and he said, "I'm sorry, the machine isn't owned by the motel. A private company installs the machines and services them once a week. And it's too late in the evening to call anybody now! There's not a thing I can do."

So I headed back to my room, but first I walked down the hall and stood in front of that stubborn machine again.

What I needed was locked inside! Have you beautiful qualities that are locked inside of you? Only you have the choice to release them! Deep within yourself you have a lot to give, but you don't know how to release your inner potential. You have a lot to offer, but something keeps you tied up—feeling timid, shy, retiring, and inferior.

I want to give you some guidelines that will help you release the dynamic potential and valuable abilities deep within you. *First*, understand that you are a decision-making creature. Where you are today is largely the result of decisions you made or failed to make! Sometimes these decisions are painful, and frequently they are risky. If you're still at the bottom of the ladder or you feel you're washed up or burned out, it's probably because of decisions you *didn't* make.

If you are discouraged because you're not more successful than you are today, it is important that you concentrate on your past successes, not on your failures.

Be led by peaks, not valleys. If you remember setbacks, you think negatively. When you surrender to a low mood, there's only one way to go, and that's down! Nobody has ever been lifted up by a down mood. Don't surrender to negative thoughts! Let that uplifting mood come! Self-confident thoughts come when you forget failures and start thinking success! *Pick a new peak and perk up!*

Where are you today? Whether you are up or whether you are down depends ultimately on your attitude. Other people may give you problems, but if you are down, it is because you have chosen to allow the problem to throw you into a down mood. *Pick a peak! Don't pick a valley!*

Put your eye on a mountaintop that will produce joy and energy and enthusiasm and excitement. Don't let a blue Monday, a blue week, or a depressing month take over your moods! You are where you are because of decisions you make. It has been established that even people who suffer from emotional depression have chosen to surrender to negative moods.

A young friend of mine was a great athlete before he broke his back. He survived, but now he walks only with crutches. Not long ago, I ran into him at a hotel.

"John," I said, "how are you?" "Lousy," he replied. "Why?" I asked. "I'm not well," he continued. "Oh, your back is still bothering you?" I prodded. "No," he quietly answered, "I'm mentally ill." "Are you really?" I questioned. "I sure am," he replied. "You don't look mentally ill to me," I enthused, "I wouldn't affirm that if I were you."

Oblivious to the crowd around us in the hotel lobby, we began to talk at length. I found that he had been programming himself negatively.

"You must never say that you are mentally ill again!" I said. "You must affirm, 'I am mentally healthy and I will be mentally healthy for the rest of my life.'"

We had dinner together that night before we went our separate ways. In the twenty-four hours from the time I met him in the lobby to the time he left, he was a transformed person. He will never be mentally ill again *unless he chooses to be!* For, before I left him, I touched him on the forehead with my finger and said, "John, anytime you feel depression coming back, you will become afraid of mental illness. Fight it by saying, 'Never again, never again, never again.'" I continued, "Affirm that you will *never again* yield to such depressing emotions." His face radiated hope and joy!

My friend chose to surrender to negative emotions— that's why he believed he was mentally ill. But now he chose to affirm the possitive. He picked a new peak. *Pick a peak!*

What thoughts would go through your head if you were seventy-seven years old and were paralyzed? Perhaps: "Well, this is it, I'm at the age when people die. It must be God's will for me to pack up. I'm only three years short of eighty. This is it!"

Not Eula Weaver! She had a stroke at seventy-seven years of age and was paralyzed, but she didn't give up. "I could hardly walk at all," she said. "Doctors gave me two choices: (1) to spend the rest of my life as an invalid, or (2) to get out of bed and start walking—no matter how much it hurt!" That's when she decided to get out and start walking. And eleven years later, and two years short of ninety, she's running a mile every day.

Her picture appeared in a newspaper. She looked attractive in her jogging suit—enjoying life, enjoying health just twelve years short of one hundred years old. *Pick a peak!*

Pick a peak! Make your decision to succeed. You may be at the bottom now because others pushed you there. But if you *stay* at the bottom, that's your decision. Nobody else's! Nobody can decide to keep you down but you, yourself. People who reach mountaintops are on the peak because they picked the peak. They made the decision to pull life together again.

A member of our television camera crew (a young Jewish lad) knows what it's like to pull himself from the bottom. He tells his story this way: "I was an unfortunate person caught in the wrong automobile at the right time. I slammed into a mountain at about seventy miles per hour. I broke two bones in my left leg and one in my right leg, suffered severe lacerations to my head and hands along with rib and lung damage. It's a miracle that I'm still alive!

"I was out of action for ten long months. Only my faith pulled me through. You must have faith—you've got to hang in there! I was lying in that hospital bed an awfully long time wondering if I would ever become a healthy young man again. All I could think about during my long recovery was the outdoors—and just being alive and well! I felt like an old man, but today I am healthy! I'm feeling good!"

I am convinced that God is unfolding a dream in your mind as you read these pages. It may be a dream to set a new goal for business. Or to pick a new peak as far as your physical fitness is concerned. Perhaps the goal you set is to improve your education. Maybe you just want to like yourself better.

Your goal may be to change your attitude toward the people with whom you work or with members of your family.

But pick a new peak today. Set new goals and make great decisions. Whether it's starting a new business or expanding your personal financial situation or climbing the ladder in your chosen profession, pick a peak that will lead you to peek to new and greater successes.

You have the freedom to choose anything you want. Why not choose love and happiness?

I close this chapter and this book using a word I seldom use: impossible. It is impossible for me to know every reader.

But, whoever you are—wherever you are—one thing I do know about you is that you have fantastic undiscovered potential waiting to be uncovered and developed.

However feeble your faith is, reach out, cry out to the God who creates life, and ask Him to give you life's most precious gift: a mountain to climb and the faith to climb it.

About the Author

Robert H. Schuller is founder and senior minister of the famed Crystal Cathedral in Garden Grove, California. His telecast, "The Hour of Power," is one of the most widely viewed programs in television history. The author of fifteen books, Dr. Schuller has received many awards and several honorary degrees. His bestselling Bantam titles are TOUGH TIMES NEVER LAST, BUT TOUGH PEOPLE DO!, TOUGH-MINDED FAITH FOR TENDER-HEARTED PEOPLE, THE BE (HAPPY) ATTITUDES, and BE HAPPY YOU ARE LOVED.